TOUR

A Journey Through Miami´s Culture

Jitney Books

https://jitneybooks.com

TOUR

A Journey Through Miami´s Culture

Pedro Medina León

Jitney Books

https://jitneybooks.com

To my mom, the most admirable human being I know.

Tour

Printed in the United States of America
Front cover art by Claudio Roncoli
Jitney books logo by Ahol Sniffs Glue
Copy edited by J.J. Colagrande
Front cover design Claudio Roncoli

Jitney Books is a Miami-based micro-publishing company focused on producing original titles by Miami-based authors writing about Miami in Miami with the intention of this material being produced into film or plays by Miami-based filmmakers or playwrights. All cover art will feature Miami-based artists.

All intellectual property rights remain with the artists and authors. Please contact publisher for media, acquisition and collaboration inquiries: jitneybooks@gmail.com
#madeindade #miamifulltime

Tour offers an overview of the main historical, cultural and popular elements that have shaped the city of Miami. Pedro Medina León shares through brief essays, chronicles and interviews, how Henry Flagler opened the doors of Miami to the rest of the country; how the decline of the legendary rock band The Doors started in Coconut Grove; how Opa Locka, a city inspired by The Thousand and One Nights, was conceived as one of the most ambitious urban projects and today is one of the poorest neighborhoods in the United States; how Bob Marley died in a hospital bed in Downtown Miami and how Cassius Clay was crowned the world boxing champion in Miami Beach. And among these fascinating and controversial characters Pedro Medina León describes the different faces of a city that started as a small agricultural and fishermen village, transformed itself into the world capital of crime and drug trafficking in the 1980s, and has now become a haven from Latin America.

Miami

I guess I think I feel alright
You come circling through the light
The skyline is bright tonight
What more perfect rendezvous?
The sundown paints the shadows through
The daylight, Amy, on what we do
It looks like darkness to me
Drifting down into Miami

Can I say
I wish that this weather would never leave?
It just gets hard to believe
That god sent this angel to watch over me
Cause my angel
She don't receive my calls
Says I'm to dumb to
To dumb to fight
To dumb to save
Well, maybe I don't need no angel at all

It looks like darkness to me
Drifting down into Miami
She could pull the sunlight through me
Coming down into Miami

Make a circle in the sand
Make a halo with your hands
I'll make a place for you to land

The bus is running
It's time to leave
The summer's gone
And so are we
So come on baby,
Let's go shut it down in New Orleans

Counting Crows

Songwriters: Adam Fredric Duritz / Ben G Mize / Charles Thomas Gillingham / Daniel John Vickrey / David A Immergluck / David Lynn Bryson / Matthew Mark Malley

INDEX

Fasten Your Seatbelts

Many of these texts started appearing in *El Nuevo Herald* during 2013, thanks to the space provided by Andrés Hernández Alene. Back then I was not even considering the idea of gathering all of them into a volume. But, little by little, and in no hurry, the folder where I kept them kept getting thicker until it reached fifty articles (some were published in different media and others were archived). Then Hernán Vera Álvarez, writer and editor — crazy book dreamer but, above all, a valuable friend that Miami has given me — gave me this idea of selecting several of them and publishing a book. At that time, I was working on another project, but things happen when they must. Therefore, between September 2017 and January 2018, I read, reread, edited, corrected and improved all my texts. I created an index that followed a certain chronology, kept balance and uniformity between the different topics, and offered the reader an overview of certain facts and characters, except for Julia Turtle and Carl M. Fisher — whom I did not incorporate, because I find their topics rather trite — for better or worse, they formed the Miami that we know today.

So, again, thank you Andrés and thank you, Hernán: please fasten your seatbelts. The Tour starts here.

ॐ

Our Man in Miami

Miami will always be in debt to Henry Flagler, who opened the doors of the city to the rest of the country and the world.

One of the most explosive scenes in *Mission: Impossible 3* takes place on a bridge. A plane fires a missile at Ethan (Tom Cruise). The rumble and its effects last almost three minutes and he ends up hanging from rubble, swaying over the turquoise open sea between Knight's Key and Little Duck Key, right across from another smaller, old and battered bridge.

Henry M. Flagler (1830-1913), founder and partner of John D. Rockefeller at Standard Oil Company — the most profitable company, until today, in the history of the United States — traveled for the first time to Florida during the 1870's. He was following a doctor's recommendations given to his wife, Mary Harkness, to settle in a tropical climate. Mary's health was fragile, and she died in 1881. In 1883, Flagler married Ida Alice Shourds and, in December of that same year, traveled to Florida on their honeymoon. Their gateway to Florida was Jacksonville, although with Ida Alice the journey lasted longer: they boarded the ferry to St. Augustine, a green city with just two thousand inhabitants. Months later, Flagler returned to St. Augustine to build the Ponce de León hotel, a Mediterranean-style hotel with five hundred and forty rooms. Flagler, a businessman, soon expanded his company and built the Royal Poinciana Hotel in Palm Beach, an area that he considered paradisiacal. The problem with Florida was transportation: The train did not go beyond Jacksonville, so it was impossible to commute to other places. If Flagler wanted his hotels to be a tourist epicenter, he had to connect the cities. So, he decided to extend the railroad route to Palm Beach.

In 1894, Florida was struck with bad weather. One of the cruelest frosts of all time killed the crops, damaging the economy dramatically. However, south of Palm Beach stretched a territory called Fort Dallas, almost uninhabited due to mosquitoes, pests and heat. Nothing interesting for many, except for Julia Tuttle, an entrepreneurial widow who sold everything in Ohio and isolated herself in these inhospitable lands. Fort Dallas was not affected by the frost, and Tuttle, who had been trying to convince Flagler to continue his railroad to Fort Dallas, got her wish. In 1895, in exchange for a portion of land, Flagler agreed to extend the railroad to Fort Dallas, a city that months later would be inscribed as Miami.

Flagler's hotel empire arrived at the Miami River shores with the Royal Palm Hotel, and consolidated Miami as a tourist attraction. Based in Miami, Flagler traveled through the Keys, the Everglades, Homestead... and, in 1905, announced what would probably be his most ambitious company — although for some it was the biggest folly that a 75-year-old man could commit. To build the Florida East Coast Railway, a hundred-and fifty-three-mile rail that would connect Miami to the south end of Florida, Key West.

The Florida East Coast Railway was done in stages between 1906 and 1912. Unpredictable weather complicated the venture: three hurricanes lashed against the coasts and blights were considerable. The biggest challenge was the seven-mile stretch between Knight's Key and Little Duck Key. The only thing that was between those two pieces of land was the Atlantic. They assessed the probability of not completing the railway, but stubborn Henry Flagler opposed it.

The Florida East Coast Railway construction concluded the morning of January 21st, 1912 and Flagler died a year later, along with his third wife, Mary Lily Kenan. Henry Morrison Flagler's project consisted of three hundred and sixty-six miles of rail linking Jacksonville to Miami and one hundred and fifty-six between Miami and Key West. A masterpiece of engineering that connected all of Florida, so unusual at the time, was rated as the Eighth Wonder of The World.

The railway continued operating after the death of Mr. Flagler. Key West became a trade window for the Caribbean and the newly inaugurated Panama Canal. Tourism was also favored. People from all over the United States traveled to the Keys and Miami for the weekend or to take the ferry to Cuba. Nevertheless, the boom lasted only until Labor Day weekend in 1935, when a hurricane swept the entire state's east coast as no other one has. The gusts of wind took hundreds of lives, homes and the impressive machine.

Little remained of the Eighth Wonder of The World. Just a few scraps, like that old seven-mile bridge, the Old Seven, Florida's historical landmark that runs parallel to the highway from Miami to Key West. And while its usefulness is limited to weekend bicycle rides or posing for camera lenses, it has also served as a stage for Tom Cruise, Arnold Schwarzenegger and James Cameron, among many others.

ↄ

Al Capone was the First One

Miami's close relationship with the mafia and illicit business dates to Al Capone's era.

One of Miami's classic urban legends claims that Al Capone used to stay at the Biltmore Hotel in Coral Gables and that his ghost still haunts the rooms in the evenings. Another urban legend, perhaps a bit more unusual, states that Al Capone closed the Clay Hotel, in the Española Way of South Beach, to place bets and do other illicit businesses.

The United States Volstead Act regulated liquor consumption between 1919 and 1933, which had a big impact on smuggling mafias. In those years, the Italian community had established itself in New York and Chicago, and with it came the mafia bosses.

Among these, the greatest of all time was Alphonse Gabriel Capone. Son of Sicilian immigrants from New York, raised in the streets of Manhattan, in his twenties, Capone was already head of the Chicago Outfit, the largest mafia syndicate in the country. The validity of the Volstead Act turned cities like New York and Chicago into hostile places for smuggling. In order for businesses to continue they needed to find new trade points such as Miami, a strategic territory with an exit to the sea, where the merchandise could keep coming in a clandestine way, in planes and boats that arrived from the Caribbean.

Al Capone made a few trips to South Florida, Cuba and the Bahamas between 1925 and 1926. In 1927, under the pretext that he needed to lead a quiet life, he moved with his son Sonny and his wife, Mae, to a mansion located in Palm Avenue´s no. 93, Miami Beach. The residence was soon recognized for its pompous parties, where guests received juicy donations. High-level public and political officials benefited from those donations, as well as students and teachers from St. Patrick's Catholic School, where Sonny studied. Al Capone´s presence in the city was controversial. Many loved him for his generosity, while others repudiated his presence. In Miami, the justice department was always following his footsteps. They tried to incriminate him on several occasions and even banned him from entering Miami Dade's jurisdiction — Miami Beach belonged to another jurisdiction. Therefore, he considered moving to Broward where he bought a piece of land in which he did not build and it was finally confiscated in 1934. Today it is a public park called Deerfield Island, which can only be accessed by boat. Despite all this, they failed to prove anything against him. He had no bank accounts under his name, nor any property. He did not write or cash any checks and all transactions were made in cash. It wasn't until 1931 when, for tax evasion, he was sentenced to eleven years in prison. Before he was incarcerated, he hid a hundred million dollars in safety deposit boxes in banks in the United States and Cuba. Those were not under his name either. He buried the keys to the boxes to recover them after walking out of jail.

He was imprisoned in 1932, first in Alabama and then in Alcatraz. When admitted he was diagnosed with syphilis and, in 1939, when he was released under medical orders, it was no longer feasible to continue his treatment. Once released, he couldn't find the keys to the boxes where he hid the money — they are still missing — and he became a fragile human being with health and mental problems. He checked himself in regularly at the hospital and health clinics and, in 1947, at the early age of 48, he died a victim of a heart attack in his Palm Avenue mansion, with his wife Mae at his side.

Regardless of the legends surrounding Al Capone in Miami, his presence was a turning point. After him, leaders of the Cosa Nostra like Santo Trafficante, Lucky Luciano and Meyer Lansky, built fortunes in Miami Beach and Havana through money laundering, illicit bets and smuggling, all overlapping under the veil of the hotel industry. The baton was then picked up by the Cuban Godfather, Jose Miguel Battle, and only a few years later came the famous 1980s and their Cocaine Cowboys.

಄

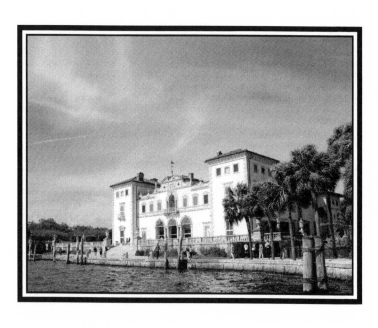

A Big House in the Jungle

Miami's most extravagant and luxurious house is located in the middle of the jungle.

Barely a decade after its foundation as a small fishing village, Miami began to capture the attention of investors and entrepreneurs. Carl M. Fisher and Mary Brickell were two of them and their names immediately stand out. James Deering's case may not be so familiar, though the legacy he left behind is.

Deering, International Harvest Company of Chicago's vice president and a 55-year-old bachelor who spent his time living between New York, Paris and Chicago, decided to spend winter seasons in Miami, trying to get away from the cold of those places. To do so, he needed to build his future residence under the supervision of someone who would share his refined and exquisite tastes. Following Mary Brickell´s recommendation he hired Paul Chalfin, a New York-based decorator and artist with studies at Harvard and the École des Beaux-Arts in Paris.

A nature lover, Deering wanted the residence to be in the jungle — in what is now Coconut Grove — on land that belonged to Mary Brickell. Thus, in 1912, after negotiations and formalizing other aspects, Deering and Chalfin left for Europe to familiarize themselves with the architectural and artistic designs of the moment. They toured France, Spain and Italy, where a Venetian villa captivated them. Later, more by Deering´s determination than from Chalfin, it was decided that the House would bear a name, a Spaniard one: Vizcaya.

Construction started in 1914 and the planned finishing date was the summer of 1915. As a source of work, it was fabulous: it employed more than a thousand people, many of whom arrived from other states. To ensure the success of this endeavor, Chalfin surrounded himself with a luxury staff: young architect Francis Hoffmann and gardening expert Diego Suárez, among others. Certain pieces, finishes and ornaments were made to order or brought from countries they had visited during his trip.

Vizcaya was Chalfin's great project and he didn't spare any expense, but construction took longer than expected. The climate did not help and neither did the swampy geography, the absence of some materials and, much less, the First World War, which delayed shipments from The Old Continent and enlisted many of the workmen in the army. In 1916, Deering departed to Paris to get away from Miami, leaving everything in the hands of Chalfin. Toward the middle of the summer of that same year, Chalfin received an ultimatum: Deering's relatives would spend the holidays in Miami, therefore, Vizcaya must be completed by December 15th. Vizcaya was delivered to Deering one day before Christmas — two and a half years after construction began — and was inaugurated with a huge party. What was not finished on that date were the gardens, which took seven more years.

Deering only enjoyed Vizcaya for a short while, as he died in 1925. A year after his death a hurricane struck the city, causing serious damage to the house. Chalfin wanted to repair it and turn it into a museum, but in 1935 it was hit by another hurricane and the damage was even worse. James Deering's nieces took over Vizcaya until 1952, when they granted the property to Miami Dade County.

Since 1953, Vizcaya is a museum open to the public, with more than two thousand pieces of art in exhibition and gardens catalogued by National Geographic as "unduplicated in America." In 1994 it was declared a National Historical Landmark.

ော

"Off to Study," Army Air Forces

During War Times, Miami is a Trench

Miami has had two key moments in its history that have changed it's facade and generated a resurgence. One is the Eighties, the Miami Vice era, and the other one is the Second World War.

On the night of May 14th, 1942, the Mexican boat *Potrero del Llano* was traveling from Tampico to New York when a German Navy torpedo hit the coast of South Florida. The resulting loss was more than ten dead and at least twenty injured, who were transported to Miami for assistance. Although the Nazis argued that it was a mistake, the Potrero was just one of many ships that sank on the coast of Florida in the early 1940s.

As in the rest of the country, hunger and misery were ravaging Florida during the Great Depression.

Also, in Florida, as an anteroom, came the first housing bubble. Major real estate projects in Miami, such as Opa Locka, Hialeah and Coral Gables, brought the price of the square meter to astronomical figures, making it quite inaccessible.

While the United States was trying to raise its head, on the other side of the Atlantic, Hitler, Hirohito and Mussolini mobilized their troops for what would be the greatest war of all time: World War II. One of the worst setbacks this country has suffered was the Japanese bombardment of the Pearl Harbor Naval Base in 1941, which served as a trigger for the country to close ranks and face the enemy. Having a vulnerable Pacific Coast, the United States preferred to mobilize a large part of its militias on the East Coast.

Soon, Miami went from being a crisis-ravaged resort city to a military barrack: the government rented four hundred hotels to accommodate seventy thousand Navy and Army officers, including famous actor Clark Gable — the King of Hollywood, who stopped filming to serve the cause. The Biltmore and Nautilus were appointed as medical centers and they installed the Homestead Air Reserve Base, a military base and pilot school, to monitor the maneuvers of German war submarines, the U-boats, off the coast of Florida. There's an anecdote about Ernest Hemingway that claims he made rounds in his own boat, *El Pilar*, to monitor the Germans, but it was just a simple pretext to go out fishing using gasoline provided by the public administration.

Fortunately, mass mobilization brought many job opportunities in agricultural, hotel and labor sectors. The unemployment rate, which had reached over 25%, fell to 1.2%, although betting and gambling also grew, as did clandestine liquor sales and prostitution. This is when the first Red Light districts appeared, too. The demographic growth experienced by Miami took it by surprise. It lost its small-town atmosphere and the government was forced to establish a rationing booklet for food and gasoline, to keep inhabitants stocked in a more balanced way.

Historians and economists argue that without the war, Miami would never have gotten ahead. This is an ongoing discussion, but what cannot be denied is that it was a vital boost that reclaimed Miami as a city, giving it back its beachfront paradise status.

℃℈

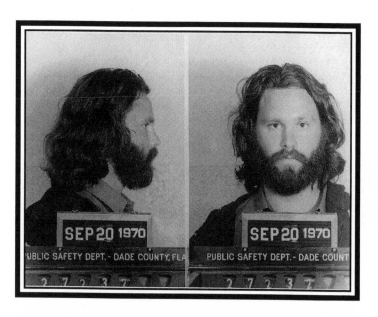

To Prudencio Agramunt Balta

The Briefest Concert

The beginning of the end of the legendary rock band The Doors, started in Coconut Grove.

On March 1st, 1969, Miami welcomed spring, although the youth´s anxiety was focused in what the Coconut Grove Dinner Key Auditorium was welcoming: the amazing rock band The Doors. 25-year-old Jim Morrison was already a damn alcoholic poet addicted to LSD who made audiences rave with "Light My Fire," "Break on Through" or "This is the End." Born and raised in Melbourne (FL), Morrison´s appearance in Miami meant his return to Florida. The conflicting relationship with his father, a Navy Admiral, forced him to finish school and move to California.

On the morning of the Coconut Grove show,

Morrison ended his long engagement with Pamela Courson and missed the non-stop flight that would bring him from Los Angeles. The next flight was a stopover in New Orleans and he arrived completely drunk. The Dinner Key Auditorium could sit approximately six thousand people, but there were so many at the box office that about thirteen thousand were waiting at the foot of the stage. The concert started at eleven o'clock with "Break on Through," in front of an impatient and uncomfortable audience due to the delay and excessive assistants. Morrison wanted to try a different format. To interact more with the public, emulating the live theaters of Los Angeles, but alcohol and drugs caused him to denigrate into insults. *"Your faces have been pressed into the shit of the world. Maybe you love it. You are all a bunch of fucking idiots."* Before finishing the fourth song, "Light My Fire" -- his incitements became intolerable: *"Hey, do you want to see my cock?"* After that they were expelled by police and security personnel. The four members of The Doors drove their limousine back to their hotel in Miami Beach and the next day they flew to Jamaica on vacation.

At that time, Miami was an Anglo, ultraconservative city which had the eyes of the press and politics over it at all times. A few months before, the Republican convention had been held at the Miami Convention Center, and Richard Nixon had won the nomination for presidential candidacy. There were protests and demonstrations during the following days, and the media denounced Morrison's behavior, accusing him expressly of unbuttoning his boot-cut jeans, lowering the zipper and showing his penis, an act which was categorically denied by Morrison and the other musicians. The news echoed rapidly across the country and it´s diminished tolerance, due to the Vietnam war. Radio stations ceased playing their songs, labels withdrew their albums from sale outlets and their concerts started getting cancelled. On March 5th, Morrison was sued for six obscenity charges. If Miami were still like this nowadays, reggaetón singers would be condemned to the electric chair.

Jim Morrison appeared before the Federal District Court of Miami Dade County on August the 12th, 1970, and on the 8th of October he was sentenced to six months in prison and a five hundred dollar fine. The verdict was appealed due to lack of forcefulness; however, after the incident, The Doors played only one more concert after which Morrison moved to Paris, where he died of a drug oversdose a year later.

Jim Morrison never received a definite verdict — after his death, the case was put aside — and in the year 2010, the governor of Florida, Charlie Crist, managed to have the charges dropped.

❧

The Greatest Of All Time (G.O.A.T.)

Miami Beach's first monument to an African-American man was erected in honor of Cassius Clay, at the Miami Beach Convention Center.

Miami Beach sunrises were altered in 1961, when an African-American man started running down the MacArthur Causeway every day at five o'clock in the morning. He was tall and sturdy. A perfect silhouette. Racial segregation was so brutal at the time, that a person of color could not walk down the street after sunset. The Civil Rights Act, which sought to put an end to this, wasn't signed until 1964.

The first time that Cassius Clay (Louisville, Kentucky, 1942- Scottsdale, Arizona, 2016) stepped into a boxing ring he was twelve years old. Since that day he knew he wanted to be a world champion and it became his priority, even more than school. His accomplishments started early. At eighteen he won a gold medal at the Olympic Games (Rome 1960). He needed a sponsor to improve his career, but boxing was considered almost only for blacks and the only one's supporting him were mobsters. Working for the Mafia was not an option. He had to knock on many doors until he finally got Louisville Group´s support.

Clay's training began in San Diego, but it didn't prosper due to a lack of understanding between him and his trainer. Then there was an opportunity to move south, to Miami, to train with Angelo Dundee, whom he fortunately knew. Cassius Clay landed at the Miami International Airport with his twenty-one years and the firm conviction of dethroning champion Sonny Liston. He settled on a motel on Biscayne Boulevard and immediately started his routine. He got up at five in the morning, jogged down the MacArthur Causeway towards the Fifth Street Gym on Washington Avenue, where he had a historic encounter with the Beatles, during the trip they made to sing on the Ed Sullivan show at the Deauville Hotel in Miami Beach, which served as a springboard for their success. He spent hours in the gym and would eat and drink frugally. While consolidating his boxing career he converted to Islam to openly fight for equality and claim the rights of his race. The Islamist leaders supported him. Malcolm X even visited Miami to spend a season with him, which cost him the respect of the community.

With nineteen fights, all in his favor, Cassius Clay challenged Sonny Liston. The fight was scheduled for February 25th at the Miami Beach Convention Hall. Liston, twelve years older than Cassius and trained at the Missouri State Prison, was sponsored by the Mafia and considered the match an audacity on Clay's behalf. Insults and threats grew between each other, although the bets were towards Liston, who was a great boxer. He was the great champion.

Clay's strategy was to physically deplete his rival and knock him out between the seventh and eighth rounds. Sonny Liston, on the other hand, went in for the kill. Cassius Clay fought against Liston and the rejection of the nearly nine thousand spectators, except a few, like Malcolm X, who was seated very close to his friend's corner. The first three rounds were for Clay, but in the fourth he began to lose his sight and Liston recuperated his points and climbed higher. It is an almost proven fact that, in the break between the third and fourth rounds, Liston ordered them to spray a poisonous substance in his gloves to blind his opponent. At the end of the fifth round Clay had recuperated and, in the sixth, lashed out in such a way that Liston asked to stop the fight before starting the seventh and fled to the hospital with a dislocated shoulder, deep wounds on his face, broken ribs and two missing teeth. Meanwhile, at the Miami Beach Convention Hall, the new heavyweight champion, euphoric and delirious, shouted to journalists and the public to eat their words.

☙

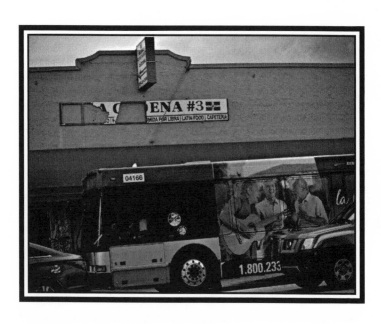

Calle Ocho

When the Cuban community consolidated in Miami, the Anglos felt that their land was being overrun and many were circulating with a sticker in their car that said, "Will the last American to leave Miami please bring the flag?".

The massive Cuban exodus to Miami began in 1959 when certain persona, unmentionable to many, tall and with a scruffy beard and military green uniform, divided Cuba's history in two. Although at first the stay in Miami was thought short and transitory, the Cuban community pretended to emulate the life and customs they left behind. They arrived at an area that was not highly valued, neighboring Coral Gables and Downtown and inhabited mostly by Jewish families. Today this area is well known as Little Havana. The businesses settled in the neighborhood were fruit shops, *bodeguitas*, laundries and many coffee shops clustered with *Guayaberas*. Toward the end of the sixties there were three hundred and sixty-nine, among which the iconic Versailles stood out, which served nearly a thousand colada cups every morning. Freshly baked bread was being sold on the streets, the Bethlehem School announced its inauguration, domino matches were held on the boardwalks and, during the evenings, a guy named Willy Chirino sang his first songs. Meanwhile, in dark bars, behind closed doors, tons of cocaine were being traded and combatants were recruited for the great retrieval of Cuba, which ended with the fateful operative known as *Bahía de Cochinos* (The Bay of Pigs).

Anglo-Local authors have debated more than once what could be "Miami's great novel" (it is still too early for Hispanics to participate in that discussion without reaching a consensus.) For the author of this book, it's *Continental Drift*, by Russell Banks, but others don't necessarily share this opinion. Les Standiford is one of the most authoritative voices to consider, with at least half a dozen fictional titles set in Miami. He compiled the *Miami Noir* short stories anthology and wrote the John Deal saga and several non-fiction books about the city. He is also the founder of the Creative Writing Program at Florida International University. In the Miami Noir prologue, Standiford sustains that one of the great novels of Miami is *8th Street*, by Douglas Fairbairn (New York, 1926-Florida, 1997).

Fairbairn, who grew up in Coconut Grove, wrote several very diverse literary works. One of them was *8th Street* (1977), a noir novel that tells the story of Bobby Mead, a *gringo* car dealership owner on 8th Street, where a brutal murder was committed against one of his employees. Since then, Mead, a victim of extortion by the Cuban mafia linked to illicit business and drug trafficking, witnessed how that community transformed the neighborhood into an extension of Havana while plotting a plan to overthrow Fidel Castro. Mead lives in the Seabreeze Hotel and must deal with the ghetto that is now South Beach because of the arrival of the Marielitos, and will also confront his daughter, who smokes joints in the bohemian hippie zone of Coconut Grove while taking her first steps as a porn star.

"Well, you live in South Beach, so you should be one thing or another, a Cuban or a Jew [...]. I think I'll be a Jew, Bobby said."

"Look, get this through your head, you are not going back to Cuba, there will never be an invasion of Cuba, the only Cuba you will ever see is the Cuba FC is going to create right here in Miami."

"Now nobody wants to come to Downtown any more. They tell you it's like coming to a foreign country."

At the time, 8th Street did not attract as much attention as his other works, for example, its memories: Down and Out in Cambridge, or the acclaimed Shoot, that Canadian director Harvey Hart turned into a movie. There were even those who questioned his credibility, but beyond the debate over Miami's great novel, 8th Street is, without a doubt, a work that has transcended time. It is one of the local literature classics.

പ

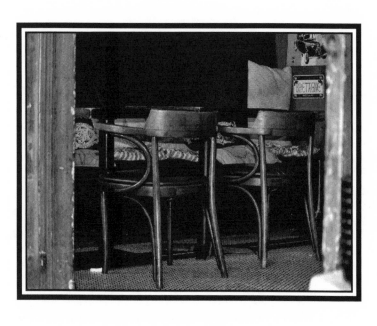

La Folie

*I lived almost nine years in South Beach and I think that
had a lot to do with my interest in learning about the city.
South Beach dazzled me from day one with its town-like
style where you can go everywhere on foot, it's minimal
streets and old houses. There were many bars, cafes and
restaurants that I visited regularly during that time, but my
favorite one was the Folie.*

One of the things I don't like about Miami is that there
are very few bohemian cafes where I can sit and read all
afternoon. Starbucks are a dime a dozen, but those coffee
factories that have colonized the city on its four sides —
and on which, by the way, I spend almost half of my
salary— are more of a mobile office for businessmen
who rotate in circles with a cellphone in their ear or for
E-Bay or *Mercado Libre* cyber-businessmen.

One of the things I love most about Miami is its ability to surprise. You can find yourself walking on Española Way after crossing a corner; a cobbled street of cracked red sidewalks that has not fallen prey to the South Beach neon, and stumble into a place like La Folie Cafe, a small corner with a soft *café pasado* aroma, an old coffee maker and the traditional noise of porcelain mugs and dishes that Miami lacks. A place as bohemian as any Montmartre groove that, as I learned after sitting several nights with the excuse of having an espresso and eating a bite, opened its doors in 2005.

Olivier Corre, the owner, pedals his bike every morning to the Folie, ready to stand behind the counter or to work as the chef. He was the one who created the menu and chose the decor: wooden tables, a bar, black and white mosaic floor and a few posters of the French Boehme on the walls. An austere and classic atmosphere, unusual in Miami, that has managed to dazzle many. More than half of the diners who attend the Folie are regulars who do not need to order what they want; some of them even go more than once a day. Although Olivier cannot recommend a favorite dish, because they are all like his children and it is not "ethical" to favor one over the other, I would venture to say that the onion soup is unbeatable. It knocks out all the others I have ever tried, and to conclude, the Printemps Roast sandwich is above standards. As far as coffee is concerned, I have only tried his *espresso* and haven´t felt the need to try anything else, since its simply magnificent.

This little piece of France that has adapted very well to Miami Beach´s palms, is open seven days a week from nine in the morning until midnight, when Olivier gets on his bike again to ride back home.

One of the things I least like about Miami is the lack of bohemian cafes. One of the things I like most is that there are very few. It is contradictory, it is true, but that´s why I enjoy them even more. They maintain that certain charm that makes me save the pages of a good novel to read during an entire afternoon, forgetting about time. For everyone else, there will always be a coffee factory just around the corner.

❧

The Film That Was Not Made in Miami

Quentin Tarantino will always have an outstanding debt with the readers of the tropical noir and Elmore Leonard books.

One of Quentin Tarantino's most indie-era films during the Nineties is *Jackie Brown* (Pam Grier), a low budget airline stewardess that colludes with arms dealer Ordell (Samuel L. Jackson) to bring illicit money into the United States through trips she makes from Mexico. The film is set in Los Angeles. Besides the trafficker and the stewardess, there is an ex-convict (Robert De Niro), a guarantor (Robert Forster) and a policeman (Michael Keaton). Before its debut, *Jackie Brown* had two weak points. It was the director's next film after *Pulp Fiction*. A resounding success that was difficult to match and it was not written by him, it was an adaptation of the

Rum Punch novel by Elmore Leonard (1925-2013), an essential reference for Tarantino´s creative universe.

Rum Punch, one of the most acclaimed novels by Elmore Leonard — as the film *Jackie Brown* is for Tarantino — is the story of an air hostess that colludes with an arms dealer. His other characters are also a guarantor, an ex-convict and a policeman, but, unlike the film, *Rum Punch*. *Rum Punch* was published in 1992, a couple of years after the last chapter of Miami Vice came on TV. More than once the characters refer to it, like when they call South Beach the *Miami Vice* Country or when Ordell wants to use guns like the ones Sonny Crockett had. It wouldn't be foolish, then, to say that the book is heir to that show, which marked a turning point in Miami and was such a strong influence on noir genre authors.

Leonard´s legacy of more than forty literary works shows a clear fascination for portraying the cities where he places them. Almost half of them, the first ones, have Detroit as their context line up with the classic Western, while nine others are set in Miami and Palm Beach, steering away from the western genre and reflecting Florida´s underworld, particularly South Beach. This occurs, for example, with the *La Brava* and *Stick* novels published in the 1980s and 1990s, in which ex-cons, failed filmmakers, Cuban assassins and Marielitos try to adapt to the pastel colors of Art Deco. Even so, despite having lived in Palm Beach for several years, Elmore Leonard was never identified as a local author.

At that time, Tarantino said in a few interviews that he had never been to Miami and that the city was too hot to film in. Maybe that's why he opted for the streets of Los Angeles whom he knew firsthand and where he had previously filmed *Reservoir Dogs* and *Pulp Fiction*, or maybe because the approach of a Californian thriller was more attractive to the film industry. For whatever reason, the fact is that the Tarantino formula worked, and his film was highly appreciated by viewers and critics. He was praised by Elmore Leonard himself. However, those of us who closely follow the noir genre, and, more specifically, the tropical noir genre, would have been interested in seeing a stronger connection between *Jackie Brown* and that delicious and brutal novel that is *Rum Punch*.

❧

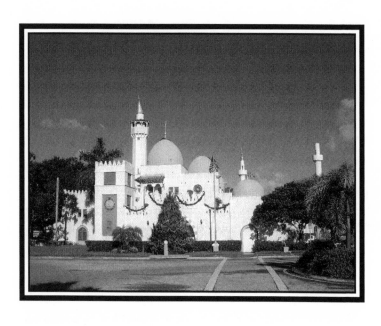

Tropical Baghdad

An ambitious Miami urban project failed. Instead, today is one of the poorest and most violent cities in the United States.

Many of the news headlines feature the city of Opa Locka. The murder of a 7/11 cashier, domestic violence, armed robbery at an ATM... Very often the year-end statistics have indicated that their crime rate is the highest in the country and, if we consider that the city is on the brink of bankruptcy, the outlook is daunting.

The Flagler railroad placed South Florida on the U.S. map. Until then, only northern territories, such as Gainesville, St. Augustine, Jacksonville, and Tampa, were benchmarks. With this occurrence, years later, in 1925, came the first big real estate boom that turned Miami into an interesting focus for investors such as Glenn Curtiss, George Merrick, Carl Fisher and James Deering. They boosted the development of cities like Coral Gables, Hialeah and Country Club Estates (today Miami Springs).

Pioneer and father of aviation Glenn Curtiss (New York, 1878-1930) designed and manufactured airplanes for the Allied army during the First World War as part of his valuable legacy. His trajectory was so prosperous that he retired at 41 and moved to Miami, searching for a quiet life. He bought several acres of inhospitable land in a territory known as Opa-Tisha-Wocka-locka, on the edge of Hialeah, where he built a ranch and fixed his residence. Although retired, Curtiss, young and ambitious, opted to join Miami´s urban development by building on his land. But he wanted a big city and he could not emulate the Mediterranean styles or Spanish villas that already characterized the others. After deliberating between different proposals and measuring the risk involved in the investment, in 1925 he decided to invest in a city inspired by the novel *The Thousand and One Nights*, an Arab concept unique in South Florida, which would be called Opa Locka.

Construction started in 1926 with the City Hall offices and some residential buildings led by the prestigious architect Bernhardt E. Muller. The first steps were a success: The City Hall was a replica of an Arab mosque and the finishes of the other buildings looked like they were taken out of a fairy tale, just as Curtiss had imagined. But the hubbub lasted only a few months. One of the most potent hurricanes in history destroyed the structures and the few finished buildings. This caused a real estate crisis and the discouragement of many of those who supported the project. Curtiss quickly got over it and didn't allow this to defeat him. He restored what was worth restoring and built new and better pieces. There was no socialite or aristocrat in the country who was not interested in that magical Arab city that was being built in Miami. Curtiss's dream began to feel real. His city was not one of the most beautiful, but it was the most impressive one.

The formal inauguration of Opa Locka took place on Saturday, January 8, 1927, with the arrival of the Orange Blossom, the most exclusive railway in the country, which traveled from New York only during winter. The opening celebration was an arabesque carnival whose guest of honor was actor Johnny Weissmuller (Tarzan). The City Hall was not finished yet but it was finished soon after, like some other hotels, plazas and houses.

However, the crisis aftermath slowed the Curtiss project. Despite all his efforts and money invested, Opa Locka wasn't being valued as he expected. He fought for two or three more years, until he lost the battle and plunged into a severe depression, dying in 1930. His Dream of Araby was buried with him.

There are few Arab structures left. City Hall is one of them. There are also vestiges of domes and arches in a few homes. Although they are continuously disappearing, in a few of the green little signs that hang from the poles at the corners of the streets it still reads: Sesame Street, Alibaba Boulevard or Sultan Avenue.

Charming Man

The first private detective that Miami ever had on the screen was played by Richard Denning, a show of thirty-two episodes from the black and white era.

Miami had a date every Friday at 10:00, during 1960 and 1961, with a tall redhead that wore an impeccable suit and a silk scarf and drank cognac with ice served in a separate glass. His office was on Flagler Street. His name was Michael Shayne and he had a sexy blond as his secretary and personal weakness.

Davis Dresser (Illinois, 1904-California, 1977), a sailor with an eye patch, was having a drink at a bar in the port of Tampico when a fight broke out. A redheaded man who was not sharing his table with anyone started punching whoever stood in his way, including Dresser. Years later, retired from the Navy and trying to make his way as an author, Dresser saw the man again in a bar in New Orleans. He was drinking alone again, in a corner table. He pulled a chair by his side and reminded him about the Tampico incident. The man excused himself, got up and never came back. That was the last time that Davis Dresser saw the man who had struck him with all his strength and courage, and that was also a trigger in the creative universe of the young author seeking good stories.

As with every great literary legend, the first Private Inspector Michael Shayne novel that Davis Dresser wrote, *Dividend on Death*, under the pseudonym Brett Halliday, though he used many more, was rejected by twenty-one editors before getting published by Seal Henry Holt & Co. After that came seventy-seven novels, more than three hundred stories, twelve movie adaptations, radio shows and the *Michael Shayne Mystery Magazine*, which was published over thirty years. In addition, Miami saw its first TV police show. Produced by NBC in black and white, under the direction of Paul Stewart, it was the hardboiled era of United States noir literature; the one with dark alleys and stairs in New York, Chicago and California´s alleyways; the Dashiell Hammett and Raymond Chandler one, to which Davis Dresser joined with one of the most iconic and unique characters of all.

Much of Dresser's stories are set in Miami. He was one of the local pioneers of this genre. More than twenty of his books were set in this city, a very different city from the one we know today, completely blonde and blue-eyed, in the midst of the post-WWII boom. *Blood on Biscayne Bay* (1943) is probably one of his most acclaimed literary works. In it, Shayne must solve the murder of a maid in a millionaire's mansion. It is a crime of passion plot with anonymous letters and poker bets at the Playmor Casino in which he relies, as in all its investigations, on his secretary, Lucy Hamilton, his contacts, Tim Rourke at the press, and Will Gentry at the Miami Police Department.

While Dresser's legacy may be one of the most extensive ones in Miami noir literature, its name tends to go unnoticed on the lists of our authors: most of them start with Douglas Fairbairn and his remarkable 8th Street or with Charles Willeford and his Inspector Hoke Moseley´s saga.

༼ঔ

The Literature District

When George E. Merrick developed Coral Gables, he never thought that, years later, that area could be considered the literature district, something that he would probably enjoy if he were alive today. The three largest and most important bookstores in the city are in that neighborhood and it is also the epicenter of most of the literary activities.

Despite the prejudices, Miami still bears the *'promised land'* label. It's always been that way. The first immigrants arrived by train in the late 1890s to a fishing village known as Coconut Grove. Its adjoining area, the Coconut Grove Backcountry, was soon to draw attention to its agricultural benefits. Solomon Merrick arrived in one of those wagons with George E. Merrick (1886-1942), his eldest son, who was thirteen at the time. The Merricks had acquired a plot of land in the Backcountry and conditioned it accordingly for the rest of the family to follow them.

George, a voracious reader who had a vocation as a poet and writer, was not enthusiastic about the trip because it meant a delay in his studies. And so, it was. For nine years he worked the land and earned his living in activities such as paving what is currently the Coral Way for a dollar a day, a task he performed with pleasure because he was fascinated with the settlers and tropical fruits and vegetables that he had never seen or tasted before. Still, his writer's soul and his devotion to reading were always a priority. At twenty-one, without any prior high school education, he was accepted at Rollins College, Winter Park, Florida. Two years later he enrolled at NYU's Law School. While studying, he devoted himself to writing and reading and earned his first publications. "The Unattainable" surfaced at the *Sandspur* magazine, and he won the New York Evening Telegram Story Contest with "The Sponger's Delilah." A letter from his father, who had little time to live, brought him back to Miami to take over the family and its agricultural businesses. By then, the Merricks were already a thriving family living in the Coral Gables Plantation area.

Enjoying prosperity and economic stability, George married Eunice Peacock in 1916 and began to ponder an idea he had for several years: to buy acres in the Coral Gables Plantation and develop an urban project. He discussed this idea with surrounding artists who, through their refined aesthetics, drew models that looked more like works of art than dwellings. That was precisely what George wanted. However, it was not until 1920, on a trip with Eunice to Havana and where he was dazzled by colonial structures, that he reaffirmed his idea. He would unify artistic beauty and architecture in an urban project called Coral Gables. That same year George achieved another of his great dreams. The Four Seas Publishing Company published his poetry book *Song of The Wind on a Southern Shore* and he shared a catalog with none other than William Faulkner.

The Coral Gables inauguration was in 1921 with twenty-six built lots that resembled small replicas of medieval terracotta castles. Since then, the Mediterranean Revival style started molding itself. A term imposed on the Italian, French and Spanish architecture and adapted to the tropical environment thanks to George's innovative ideas. The inauguration was such a success, that in six days they sold three hundred lots. Coral Gables growth was exponential, four years later it was inscribed in public records and consolidated as one of the most important urban projects in the United States.

Florida's first major real estate boom, in 1925, was the result of this phenomenon.

As we all know, endings are not always happy. In 1926, a devastating hurricane paralyzed the real estate business and Merrick's economy suffered setbacks. He drowned in alcohol, which almost cost him his marriage, until the Great Depression brought the final collapse, including the Steering Committee expulsion of his own project. Tired of trying in vain to get ahead, George and Eunice moved to Matecumbe Key, broken, and he took refuge in writing. Since then, George E. Merrick disappeared from the Coral Gables scene and only returned in 1940, a few years before he died, as a post office clerk.

ɛ⌃ɔ

WANTED BY THE FBI

ANDREW PHILLIP CUNANAN

*UNLAWFUL FLIGHT TO AVOID PROSECUTION -
SECOND DEGREE MURDER*

Alias: **ANDREW PHILLIP DE SILVA**

Photo taken about 4/97

Date of Birth: **AUGUST 31, 1969** Race: **WHITE** Sex: **MALE**
Height: **5'9''-5'10"** Weight: **160-180 LBS** Eyes: **BROWN**
Hair: **DARK BROWN**

Cunanan may wear prescription eyeglasses. He has been known to
change hairstyle and weight. He has portrayed himself as being wealthy.

CAUTION

CUNANAN IS BEING SOUGHT FOR AN APRIL 1997 MURDER IN
MINNESOTA, AND FOR QUESTIONING IN FOUR OTHER MURDERS
INCLUDING THE JULY 15TH KILLING OF DESIGNER GIANNI VERSACE, IN
FLORIDA. CUNANAN MAY BE IN POSSESION OF A HANDGUN.

ARMED AND EXTREMELY DANGEROUS

IF YOU THINK YOU HAVE INFORMATION ABOUT THIS MAN, CALL
THE **FBI (313) 965.2323**
OR
TRIANGLE FOUNDATION AT: (313) 537.3323

ADDITIONAL INFORMATION AT FBI WEB SITE: http://www.fbi.gov/mostwant/cuna.htm

The Most Glam Murder

The regular inhabitant of Miami usually attributes the assassination of Gianni Versace to one of his scorned or frustrated ex-lovers. However, to date, the authorities have never been able to prove that this is true.

It took Miami ten years to turn the page of that harrowing eighties decade that marked it for life. However, on the morning of July 15, 1997, two bullets brought that decade back to the police station.

The first murder that Andrew Cunanan (California, 1969-Miami, 1997) committed took place in Minneapolis. His victims were David Madson and Jeff Trail. Cunanan, a con-artist to entrepreneurs with money and social status, referred to Madson as the love of his life, someone who he wanted to marry. It is presumed that the cause of murder was jealousy. The trail was found at Madson´s apartment; a skull pierced by a hammer. A few days later, Madson's body showed up on the grass, in the street. Thereafter, Cunanan began a journey in Madson´s Jeep. His next stop was Chicago, where the next victim would be 70-year-old Lee Miglin, with whom he was never linked. He then traveled to New Jersey, where he claimed the life of forty-five-year-old William Reese, whom he did not know. By then, Cunanan's face was already featured in the press as one of the FBI's most wanted. Everything suggested that New York would be his next destination, but he was only there a few days, trying to go unnoticed. He then took off to the southernmost paradise of United States, Miami Beach. He arrived in mid-May, under the name Andrew Da Silva, and stayed at the Normandy Plaza. There, he had no qualms about frequenting gay clubs, casting for gay pornography and living like any other passerby. But the FBI's Most Wanted post betrayed him on every corner and the authorities soon received alerts about his presence.

Miami´s resurgence during the early 1990s attracted the world's interest. The Art Deco and pastel colors, well vindicated by Sonny Crockett in *Miami Vice*, managed to get artists and celebrities to set up their residence in Miami Beach. One of those celebrities was designer Gianni Versace who, in

1992, with his partner Antonio D'Amico, acquired a Mediterranean Revival style mansion in the then splendorous Ocean Drive which they redecorated and called the *Casuarina*. It was unusual to find Versace in the neighborhood. In the mornings he would send one of his assistants in search of newspapers. But on July 15th he decided to walk to the News Café, one of his favorite places, going incognito amongst the diners who, before spending their day at the beach, order a cup of coffee and buy some magazines.

Then, back at the *Casuarina*, he was hit at the door by someone he had never seen before. Andrew Cunanan pulled the trigger of the 40 caliber Taurus twice. It was the same gun that had killed William Reese, entering Versace´s brain and face and bathing the sidewalk and the coral steps with blood. As they took Versace to Jackson Memorial Hospital, where he would be declared clinically dead, Cunanan was scurrying away through the alleyways with the coldness of a person who had murdered five people in less than four months.

On July 24th, the sound of a gunshot inside a boathouse alerted the neighborhood. When the Miami Beach Police Department arrived, they found serial killer Andrew Cunanan dead, with the same Taurus that had killed Versace by his side.

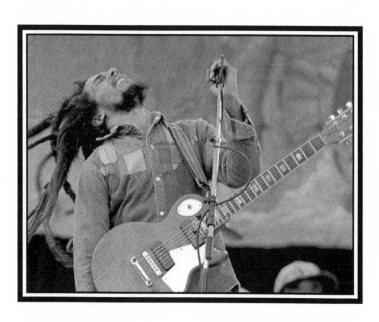

Homeland to The Rastafarian

Biographies and reports often show a very strong link between Bob Marley and London or New York but make very little reference to his transcendental relationship with the city of Miami.

Those of us who cut ties with our countries feel that the "new homeland" becomes the place where our loved ones are. That is why, if we were to choose where to die, it would certainly be there, surrounded by those people.

Bob Marley reached the peak of his career in Europe between 1975 and 1977, while living in London. He managed to become the first Third World musician with an international impact similar or greater than artists like Mick Jagger. His zenith began with the Exodus tour, which sold out in England, Holland, Denmark, France, Belgium, Germany and Sweden. The United States was not indifferent to his music, though, compared to Europe, it had a notable disadvantage. The great American Exodus tour was scheduled to start after the European one, but things do not always go as planned. In France, while playing football against a team of journalists, Marley broke a toenail and the wound was severe. His doctor found cancer cells and recommended amputating the toe to prevent the spread of cancer. The Exodus tour was cancelled and that year, 1977, Marley would fly to Miami for a second medical opinion.

The city that Marley visited was quite different from the one we know now. It was not populated by southern Latin Americans, but by the third world Caribbean countries, the Bahamas, Haiti, Jamaica and Aruba. Legal immigration and the human smuggling boats that arrived from Haiti and the Bahamas were a daily occurrence. Fidel Castro's dictatorship was increasingly consolidating a Cuban community that had always had a presence in South Florida, although initially for other reasons, the nonconformity with the Batista government or the luxury that a certain elite could afford to live in both places at the same time.

In Miami, the panorama was not very encouraging for Marley. Doctors at Cedars of Lebanon Hospital (Downtown Jackson Memorial today) confirmed the diagnosis. The cancer cells had to be removed immediately and the best thing was to amputate the toe. That was not an option for the Rastafarian creed, but it did allow for the removal of cells. Marley bought a house to rest during the postoperative period and settle in with his wife Rita and Cedella Booker Marley, his mother, who lived in Delaware and moved with them. A couple of months later, and somewhat recovered, he finished writing Kaya at the Criteria studios on Biscayne Boulevard. His famous hit "Buffalo Soldier" was also recorded there. Having a wife, mother, house and children in Miami, his plans continued consolidating there. He had almost two years of glory with the albums Survival, Uprising and Kaya (a tour that culminated with a concert at the Jai Alai Arena in Miami). But in New York, during the Uprising tour, the cancer raised its ugly head again. Marley traveled to see his doctor in Germany, but this time there was no truce. He had only a few days left to live. He returned to Miami, to his house, to spend his last moments with his family. On Monday, May 11, 1981, at 11:45 a.m., Bob Marley passed away holding his mother's hand, at the Cedars of Lebanon Hospital.

The fact that the biographical and documentary texts devote only a few lines to this passage of his life, contextualizing it more between London, Germany and New York, and affirming that his death in Miami was circumstantial, is totally rebuttable. The utmost epitome Rastafarian was a regular on these streets. Even one of his most popular photos, in which he is playing soccer, was taken at a park in Miami. Although in Germany he was given a few days to live and was able to stay there, he boarded a plane and "took his last bow" in the world capital of bikinis and silicone. Today, several of his children live here and Cedella, his mother, stayed here since the end of the seventies until her death in 2008.

ℭ

A Noir in Pastel Colors

While Miami Vice was decisive, because it defined the style of the city — Miami was not as it was portrayed in the show —, that was not its only contribution. In addition, it marked a turning point in local noir literature.

At the end of the first half of the 1980s, Miami was populated with immigrants from the lowest social strata in Latin America. It had the highest murder rate in the United States and was the epicenter of the Drug Cartel Operations. It was no longer the gentle resort of the elderly, or the tourist destination of many. People preferred vacationing in the Bahamas and other Caribbean islands. However, on September 28, 1984 the *Miami Vice* show was broadcast on TV, a show that, sooner rather than later, reinvented the city and further promoted it´s continuous fall.

With a 1.3-million-dollar budget for each show, this series, created by Anthony Yercovich and produced by Michael Mann, featured two undercover police officers: James Sonny Crockett (Don Johnson) and Ricardo Rico Tubbs (Philip Michael Thomas) in their fight against drugs, prostitution and illegal business.

While the protagonists were Crockett and Tubbs, the action focused more on Crockett. He walked in first every time they opened a door, drove the car or the boat when they pursued someone and, in general, we knew more details about his life than Tubbs.

Crockett drank, he was tough, violent, unstable, divorced and a womanizer. A character whose profile differs little from a hardboiled inspector, but Yercovich and Mann bet on a twist to the classic character and placed Crockett´s home in a boat, with a crocodile as a pet. They dressed them with a jacket, white trousers and sleeveless T-shirts. He wore espadrilles without socks, the perfect tan and modeled Carrera sunglasses while riding his black Ferrari.

Miami Vice´s episodes were not set as traditional noir stories are, in plush bars, sinister backrooms and dark alleys. They unfolded in broad daylight, in mansions, drinking cocktails among bikinis and pools and showing off the Art Deco splendor of Miami Beach, although the lumpen had the same nature as that of the dark alleys.

In the eyes of the world, *Miami Vice* stamped the noir city name to Miami. However, the genre already had significant presence in its literature. Between the Sixties, Seventies and early Eighties, John D. MacDonald and Charles Willeford wrote literary works that are considered classic in the canon today. Leslie Charteris, Brett Halliday and Douglas Fairbairn also left us notable books.

Since then, noir has continued to consolidate in local writing. There are few authors based here who write it, perhaps Les Standiford — with John Deal´s saga — and Carl Hiassen are the most representative, although there are many more, like James W. Hall and Lynne Barrett. There are also great writers like Tom Wolfe and Charlie Smith who, without being part of this environment, have ventured to tread the ground. What is interesting is the amount of these stories that keep the marginal good noir, the purest hardboiled, but also include the glamour that only Miami offers - and that *Miami Vice* made its own, with Fisher Island mansions, yachts, open ocean sunsets at Biscayne Bay, daiquiris and Brickell's aquamarine skyline. John Deal, Standiford saga´s detective, is a real estate character who drives a sports car, and one can easily imagine him wearing Crockett's espadrilles or dressing in his white jackets.

For *Miami Vice's* 30-year anniversary the newspapers and magazines published articles that, from different approaches, said the same thing: "*Miami Vice* marked a turning point in the history of Miami." This is an undeniable fact, but it is nothing more than a paraphrase of what, at the time, journalists like David Rieff and T. D. Allman captured so well in their books *Going to Miami* and *Miami. City of the future.* What has not been attributed to Yercovich and Mann is the fabulous contribution they made to literature. They created a noir with their own patent while setting new play rules on the board of our narrators. The rules of a pastel-colored noir.

❧

La Brava, South Beach

In addition to violence and chaos, the decade of
The Eighties brought a prolific time of great literary
workmanship to Miami.

Elmore Leonard´s (1925-2013) didn´t like it when his editor, Marguerite Harper, advised him to stop writing Western novels as they were no longer successful for the publishing market. The Charles Dickens of Detroit, as they called him for his particular ability to recreate that city and its speech, had at least a dozen westerns set there that had consecrated him as one of the great representatives of that genre.

While *Miami Vice* was responsible for portraying the most violent times of the city to the universal arena, there were also other less popular manifestations, such as literature, that described what was being lived. Perhaps the saga of private detective Hoke Moseley, by Charles Willeford, has been the most significant, though not the only one. Elmore Leonard, who moved from Detroit to Palm Beach and frequented Miami, took the leap from Western to noir in Florida, turning into one of the authors who left his legacy there. His books, *Stick*, *Glitz* and *La Brava*, published between 1982 and 1985, are notable frescoes of the underworld not cast by the classic inspector or marginal detective. His characters are rather swindlers, ex-cons and unemployed men who are looking for money through truculent businesses, drug dealers and extortion lenders.

La Brava is probably one of Leonard's most outstanding works. In his pages, Joe La Brava, a Secret Service ex-agent now working as a photographer, goes after a car thief in South Beach. The criminal, Cundo Rey, is a newly arrived Marielito from Cuba who also makes a nightly living as a naked dancer at a strip club on the beach. The cast with whom La Brava and Rey alternate are a former actress with a short cinematographic career, an ex-police officer with little affinity for the Latin Americans who are starting to occupy "their territory" and an addict who uses a stolen wheelchair. In La Brava the characters drink and snort cocaine, and there is explicit sex in an atmosphere of dubious bars, motels and cafes located on Collins Avenue and Ocean Drive. This sordidness is managed with exquisite literary resources, such as the sharp and direct dialogue in which the conflict between English and our language is already surfacing.

Martin Scorsese, Dustin Hoffman and Elmore Leonard met at a hotel in Manhattan to discuss taking *La Brava* to the big screen. On several occasions, Hoffman had expressed interest in playing the photographer and Scorsese in directing the film, but the meetings lead nowhere. Leonard left New York in disgust and said that he had not been paid for this wasted time. There were some attempts to revive the project, with other producers, but Joe la Brava never made it to the screen.

Elmore Leonard passed away at 87 with more than forty titles published, more than thirty film and television adaptations, and is recognized as "the father of the new American noir."

℘

Scarface: Everybody Loves the Bad Guy

One of the local cinema classics is Scarface. The film, starring Al Pacino, defined a new era and a new immigrant profile.

One of the bestselling souvenirs at Washington, Ocean Drive and Collins Avenues stores is The *T-shirt* with Tony Montana's face and the legend *"The World is Yours."* Montana, whose role was played by Al Pacino in the Brian de Palma movie Scarface, is a popular icon in Miami.

Scarface is one of de Palma's *Greatest Hits*. It's starting point is the historical exodus of the Mariel. Between the months of April and October of 1980, Fidel Castro sent nearly 125,000 Cubans to take refuge in Florida, emptying prisons and mental institutions on the island. Brian de Palma recreated Tony Montana as one of those refugees, a vulgar, ordinary, ambitious fellow who soon became Miami's number one narco-trafficker. The film is monotonous, with no further argument than snorting cocaine, laundering money and firing weapons. If we´d spent the three hours that *Scarface* lasts in front of the screen today, we would definitely say that it's not worth the effort. It is a film that has not aged well and, setting aside Al Pacino´s masterful performance, it´s shocking to see a Marielito interpreted by an actor who does not speak Spanish. If it would have been filmed nowadays, Montana would have been played by Ricardo Darín, Diego Luna or Gael García Bernal. But we mustn't throw it all away. Remember that Miami, in those years, was no less sordid or petty than how it was represented in the film. The murder rate was the highest in the country (six to seven per day), at least one of the bills in every Miami wallet had been used for snorting cocaine and the cultural clash between Anglos and Latinos was untenable. Alex Daoud, Miami Beach´s mayor in 1985, tells in his *Sins of South Beach* memoirs how he went out at night with cops to hunt *Latins* and beat them up.

De Palma´s *Scarface* is a remake of *Scarface* by Howard Hughes, a 1932 film in black and white which has little to do with the Marielitos and Miami. It is about the early years of Al Capone on the streets of Chicago. Hughes´ *Scarface* is the adaptation of a novel that bears the same title, signed by "a such" Armitage Trail in 1929.

Towards 1920, when *hardboiled* genre was at its peak, there was a certain rumor spreading among the pulp magazines about a sixteen-year-old boy using the Armitage Trail pseudonym. Behind Trail hid Maurice Coons (1902-1930), a teenager that, at fifteen, left school to devote himself to writing because he wasn't interested in anything else. Coons spent part of his youth on the streets of Chicago, moving in the shadows, dazzled by the Sicilian Mafia. At that time, The Chicago Outfit was at its peak and Al Capone was already known within the organization. According to an urban legend, it was during those years when, coming out of a bar, Capone received two knife wounds in the face, giving him his nickname: *Scarface*.

So, both myth and legend, Al Capone served as inspiration to Maurice Coons novel *Scarface* about Tony Guarino's story, a gangster who started operating in Chicago and turned out to be the biggest mobster in America. The 156-page novella, which yields a small but great homage to Capone albeit with a not so happy ending, was acclaimed by readers and critics and the author soon sold the rights to turn it into a screenplay. Fame and recognition leave a good taste in your mouth. Coons knew this first-hand. He was soon seen in luxury cars with a chauffeur, drinking often and eating at good restaurants. That *Bon Vivant* facet, however, came with a price. A heart attack took Coons at 28, weighing over three hundred pounds. He failed to see the adaptation of his novel (Al Capone, yes).

In addition to *Scarface*, Armitage Trail wrote *The Thirteenth Guest* and, despite his short life, his literary contribution transcended time and today he is recognized as one of the essential pioneers of the United States hardboiled genre.

ℰℐ

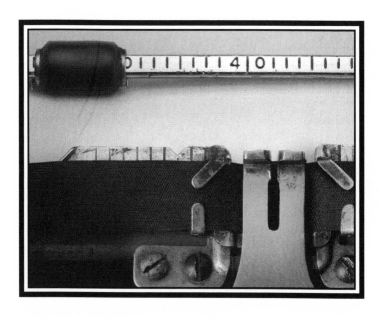

Charles Willeford's Shadow

One of the authors who most influenced local noir
contemporary narrators is Charles Willeford.

Miami's brief literary history is no more than sixty or seventy years old, though it was only until the eighties that it started to shape its actual characteristics, the noir genre and cultural clash stories. Russell Banks´s *Continental Drift* surfaced in 1985, a novel that, without exaggeration the author of this book considered it "Miami's Greatest Novel." Then, in 1987, from the non-fiction genre, T. D. Allman published *Miami, City of the Future*, perhaps the most effective book to understand the city. But Charles Willeford marked a turning point in Miami´s literary path between 1984 and 1988, when he published detective Hoke Moseley´s novels, comprising *Miami Blues* (1984), *New Hope for the Death* (1985), *Sideswipe* (1987) and T*he Way We Die Now* (1988).

Like all Miami inhabitants, Willeford was not born in Miami. He arrived in the Nineteen Sixties. He was forty-one and had traveled through the United States, France and Peru. He studied English Literature at the University of Miami, so he could become a teacher at Miami Dade College.

Despite having written nearly twenty titles under his name, he did not gain great literary recognition –his books were in the catalog of small publishing houses- until Hoke Moseley´s saga, set during the harrowing decade of the 1980s in Miami. Moseley is a divorced, heavy drinking, dirty-street policeman who lives at a Miami Beach hostel. It´s set mostly among Mexicans, Cubans, gang members, drug traffickers and undocumented Haitians. However, the value of his work, in addition to its literary quality, is that the detective faces the Latin American culture and a city that he can't entirely understand but must accept in order to adapt to his surroundings. Every day there are more police officer colleagues who´s surnames are Perez and Sanchez, as his partner Ellita´s, a Cuban whom at first, he looked down on but ended up becoming his roommate.

There is no doubt that Miami shocked Willeford. He unveiled a city hitherto unbeknown that had absolutely nothing to do with its marketed image through his Hoke Moseley novels. Little has changed. Our storytellers, from the most commercial ones in English (such as Carl Hiaasen or Les Standiford), to the most Indie ones in Spanish, *Viaje One Way: antología de narradores de Miami*, recreate the city. Sometimes noir, sometimes with a cultural friction, but in both cases, hostile and difficult to understand. They also exhibit a very different city than the one you know.

Willeford died of a heart attack in 1988, without suspecting that he was establishing the first bases of the literary identity of a city that, twenty-five years later, has not fully consolidated itself, but is on its way of doing so. The fifth book of the Moseley Saga was never published. It remained a manuscript. *Miami Blues* was brought to the screen in 1990 and, although it was not a great success, is considered as one of Miami´s classic films.

To talk about the father of Miami´s literature would be very ambitious, but it is fair to say that the shadow of Charles Willeford is among the pages of our authors.

Hotel, Sweet Hotel

On November 23, 1981, Time magazine published a cover that read "Paradise Lost?" over the Florida map with a sad sun. During the eighties, Miami hit rock bottom.

In April of 2017 headlines read that the last of the Cocaine Cowboys, Gustavo Gus Falcón, Willy Falcón's younger brother, had been arrested in Orlando while riding a bicycle with his wife, after being a fugitive for twenty-six years. Falcón was sought in Mexico, Colombia and other Latin American countries, but he never left the United States. He only changed his identity and moved to the north of Miami with his family.

In the late 1970s and early 1980s, Miami was recognized on the U.S. map as a drug and crime capital. The brutal cold-blooded massacre at the Dadeland liquor store occurred at that time. The morgue collapsed, and corpses had to be piled in Publix shopping carts. McDonald's didn't have any coffee spoons left because they were ideal for snorting the "white magic powder." The curtain of that "horror movie" was unveiled at the Mutiny Hotel in Coconut Grove, an area that was known as the bohemian neighborhood. On the deck of the Mutiny, a terrace overlooking the bay, celebrities such as Led Zeppelin, Liza Minelli, Julio Iglesias, the protagonists and producers of Miami Vice, Cat Stevens and many others met amongst endless platinum blondes and Dom Perignon parties -it was the place where more was sold in the country- *I did a movie called life, with actors that were real people,"* says Burton Goldberg, former owner of the Mutiny. *"We had dictators, secret police, drug people, bankers, the international trade, gunrunners, and celebrities: Rod Serling, Senator Kennedy, Cher, Hamilton Jordan, Jacqueline Onassis, George Bush. Mimes and magicians! Naked dancers in very fine taste, not prurient! Music! Chairs with enormous arms!* Sean Rowe. Article by Sean Rowe, published in the Miami New Times. October 6, 2005.

In addition to the jet set, since the hotel opened its doors in 1968, it served as the Cuban mafia's quarters. A mafia banished by Fidel Castro who, once in power, eradicated the casinos, cabarets and hotels that degraded the island. Little by little, former Bay of Pigs militia, Marielitos and operation Pedro Pan emigrants also joined their ranks.

From the narco-trafficker, mobster and pimp mosaic frequenting that deck, a long list of criminals emerged. Among them, two young Miami senior high school dropouts, Guillermo Willy Falcón and Salvador Sal Magluta. Barely twenty-one, Sal and Willy, who were smuggling tons of cocaine, drove their racing boats and didn't hesitate when wielding a revolver, positioned themselves among the most important drug lords in Florida and the world.

That was Sal and Willy's glory decade. Their organization, "Los Muchachos Corp," was a direct link between Escobar and the Colombian cartels of Miami. The organization funded CIA attacks against Fidel Castro, acquired properties (in cash) for over two trillion dollars and smuggled approximately seventy-five tons of coke.

While the war on narcotrafficking was causing alarm for a long time, in 1988, George H. Bush and his administration started big operations with the DEA and the CIA to combat it in Miami. The beginning of the end of "Los Muchachos" came in 1991, with their arrest. The trial was one of the most significant in national history. It was known as "The Estates vs Los Muchachos," and it took place until four years later, as it was very difficult to incriminate them because they killed witnesses and bought judges and prosecutors. Sal Magluta is serving a 195-year sentence, while Falcón served a 20-year one and his lawyers are still fighting to prevent his deportation to Cuba (he never became a U.S. citizen).

The constant presence of the CIA, DEA, Miami Police Department and constant scandals diminished The Mutiny's charm. The total loss of glamour was brought upon by the concurrence of the Marielitos who emulated the hero of the moment: Tony Montana, from Scarface. In 1989, a real estate group acquired the property to build a European-style boutique hotel condo.

 confidante

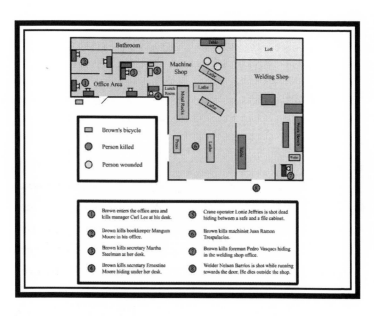

Legend:
- ☐ Brown's bicycle
- ● Person killed
- ○ Person wounded

Floor plan labels: Bathroom, Machine Shop, Loft, Welding Shop, Office Area, Lathe, Table, Metal Racks, Lunch Room, Press, Work Bench, Vault, Welder

1. Brown enters the office area and kills manager Carl Lee at his desk.

2. Brown kills bookkeeper Mangum Moore in his office.

3. Brown kills secretary Martha Steelman at her desk.

4. Brown kills secretary Ernestine Moore hiding under her desk.

5. Crane operator Lonie Jeffries is shot dead hiding between a safe and a file cabinet.

6. Brown kills machinist Juan Ramon Trespalacios.

7. Brown kills foreman Pedro Vasques hiding in the welding shop office.

8. Welder Nelson Barrios is shot while running towards the door. He dies outside the shop.

The Great Massacre

Hight School teacher Carl Robert Brown is the biggest murderer in the city of Miami.

The afternoon of April 20th, 1982, fifty-one-year-old Carl Robert Brown wore a Panama hat over his almost bald head and pedaled his bicycle near the Miami River, at the height of Northwest 17th Street when he was rammed by two subjects who shot him at point blank range with a .38 Caliber pistol. A group of police patrols with their blue and red sirens showed up and the murderers, Ernest Hammett and Mark Kram, said they had fired the gun because a few minutes before Brown had opened fire and killed several people at Bob Moore's Welding and Machine Shop, located a couple of blocks away.

The violence of the eighties was a turning point for Miami. Crimes perpetrated by Colombian cartels —the bloody shooting at the door of Dadeland Mall — and the famous riots and racial street brawls were not any different from those portrayed in today's headlines. They made the city lose its resort or winter barracks label for the Anglos that came from New York, Washington or Virginia, to spend the coldest months of the year. But beyond these issues that the sensationalism had turned into movies and television series, hostility was lived on every scale, in every corner.

Carl Robert Brown moved to Miami in 1955, after being discharged from the navy. He studied education at the University of Miami (UM) and devoted himself to teaching at Hialeah Jr. High School. Brown came to South Florida from Chicago and found a not-so-small Afro-American community, and a Latin American one that grew exponentially and began to overshadow the Anglos. During Brown's employment at Hialeah Jr. High, racial issues soon manifested among his students, who repeatedly denounced his racist (and even sexist) comments and offenses. To lessen the mood, Brown was transferred to Drew Middle School, a fact that served little to alter his behavior: only a few months later, he was denounced once again. After analyzing the allegations against him, the school principal ordered him to temporarily suspend labors due to mental imbalance and seek treatment. His doctor would have to approve his reinstatement.

The morning before Hammet and Kram killed Brown — who already had the psychiatrist's release and would soon return to school — Brown had gone to Bob Moore's Welding and Machine Shop to have a lawn mower engine installed on his bicycle, to increase its power. The service fee was twenty dollars and Brown considered that to be excessive. After an altercation with the manager he withdrew after threatening he would return to settle the issue. So, it was that, the next day, almost at lunch time, Brown showed up at Bob Moore's armed with an Ithaca rifle. First, he entered the offices and shot three victims. Then he went through the work areas and shot eight more. With twenty more cartridges in his pocket, he put his hat on and went out in search of his bicycle. Hammet and Kram were not sentenced for killing Brown, nor was it clear who pulled the trigger: They argued that both shot at the same time and the forensic statements indicated that Brown may have suffered from schizophrenia.

The killing at Bob Moore's Welding and Machine Shop is considered, at the moment of writing this book, the largest mass murder ever committed by a person in the history of Miami.

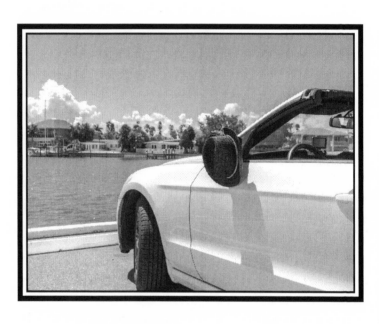

The Blues

The Hollywood film industry took an interest in Miami towards the end of the 1980s and early 1990s, when the city ended one of the most critical decades of its history.

Culture clash, violence and drugs denigrated the city in the 1980s. It was in the middle of that decade, with the help of the *Miami Vice* show that its resurgence began. People started seeing it as an Art Deco paradise and the whole country had their eyes on Miami. Hollywood was no exception: in the nineties, it served as a stage for almost twenty films (more movies were shot during this period than in any other). Probably the most outstanding ones were *Donnie Brasco, Any Given Sunday, There's Something About Mary, The Birdcage, Striptease, Ace Ventura* and *Bad Boys.*

The first director to bet on Miami was George Armitage, in 1990, with *Miami Blues*. This film is the story of Junior (played by Alec Baldwin), a San Quentin State Prison ex-convict looking to start a new life in South Florida, but that new life didn't necessarily mean getting away from crime. On the contrary, Junior sets his new headquarters for robberies, murders and scams here. *Miami Blues* could have been the heir forebearer to Miami Vice since it takes full advantage of the Biscayne Bay and aquamarine crystal skyline. Somehow, Junior resembles Sonny Crockett's prototype, but in a bandit version: handsome, perfectly tanned, pastel-colored attire and a dandy manner, although he lives in the beautiful neighborhood of Coral Gables and not on a boat and he lunched at The Venetian Pool. Armitage´s film is an adaptation of Charles Willeford´s book *Miami Blues* and a jewel of the Noir literature, Armitage´s favorite genre (he also directed *The Big Bounce*, based on Elmore Leonard´s novel).

It is difficult for a film adaptation to encompass all aspects of a literary work, but the *Miami Blues* film, which does not give Hoke Moseley any limelight, is very different from the Charles Willeford one. George Armitage probably rescued what was least interesting to the author to represent on his pages and bet on the Miami Vice formula that had already worked well. The truth is that, while Wilford's book transcended, Armitage's was pleasantly received by the audience, but did not achieve any greater recognition.

ᘓ

Days in Paradise

The relationship between the Beatles and Miami was one of love at first sight.

....

The first Beatles album started playing in America at the end of 1963, under the name *Beatlemania! With The Beatles*, and in early 1964, their song "I Want to Hold your Hand" was at the top of the billboard charts. *With The Beatles* was the Groups' second album, although in Europe, where they were already very popular, it came out under a different title. Their first foray into the United States came months later, with the *A Ticket to Ride* tour. They played in twenty-three cities and even Canada. *Beatlemania! With The Beatles* surfaced there before it did in the USA. This tour was remembered as the greatest Rock ' n Roll tour of all time and became the representation of the

influx of British music into the American market – The British Invasion. After that, they did a few more smaller tours.

A Ticket to Ride was not the official landing song of the Beatles in North America. Their manager, Brian Epstein, organized a mini-tour in New York, Washington D.C. and Miami to study the public and media reaction. The concerts at Carnegie Hall in Manhattan, New York, and at the Coliseum Theater in DC, were massive successes. They were interviewed on the Ed Sullivan show in New York, during prime time. The last stretch was reserved for Miami. Here they would offer a small performance at the hotel where they were staying, the Deauville, in Miami Beach, also as part of the Ed Sullivan Show. Both episodes of the Sullivan Show reached a total of 150 million viewers.

The Liverpool quartet landed in Miami on Sunday, February 13th, on a simple domestic commercial flight. More than five thousand people were waiting for them at Miami International Airport, Concourse No. 3. The room was overcrowded and several of the windows were broken. Some attendants suffered physical damage and asphyxiation. The Beatles were not expecting this massive welcome, as Paul McCartney told journalist Larry King. Mr.

King was the only American reporter invited to cover the entire *A Ticket to Ride* tour. Neither the press nor the police had expected the welcome. But at that time, these four 20-year-old childish looking guys with disheveled hair, not yet popular in the local mainstream, arrived with an anti-war and anti-racial segregation message. The United States was going through a critical stage in this regard, nourished by the counterculture youth in San Francisco. It is not a coincidence that *A Ticket to Ride* was the song that opened the tour in this city, as their way of protesting war actions in Vietnam. Here, in the Bohemian neighborhood of Coconut Grove, in Peacock Park, rose a community similar to a "little San Francisco" one, as previously mentioned, was covered by a marijuana cloud, long manes, wispy beards, guitars and drums. The nation, on the other hand, was mourning President Kennedy's assassination, which took place during November 1963, and the youth fully identified with the band's message.

Apart from the small performance of only 6 songs, and a few official dinners, the Beatles spent their time in the pools and the ocean, staying in direct contact with the huge number of fans that constantly asked for autographs – therefore the many "I met the Beatles in person" anecdotes in Miami. The city was caught in the heat of the John Lennon,

George Harrison, Paul McCartney and Ringo Star fever. *The boys*, as they were called in inner circles, took boat rides, drank cocktails, reveled in the bikinis, toured the city and visited Muhammad Ali who was training at the Fifth Street Gym on Alton Rd, preparing for his fight against Sonny Liston at the Miami Convention Center. There Ali would be crowned World Champion, a triumph he could not celebrate in Miami Beach. Jim Crow´s laws of racial segregation forbade him to do so.

For these boys, who were used to the grey and cold of London, the tropics turned out to be a paradisiacal and dazzling place, as reflected today in collection of pictures hanging at the Betsy Hotel´s hallways. This confirmed to Epstein what his intuition was already saying: *the boys* were to return soon and with a greater commitment. The Beatles did not return to Miami, but to the Gator Bowl Stadium in Jacksonville, with their *A Ticket to Ride* tour, under the condition that African Americans could attend, since they were originally not allowed.

Set list, Hotel Deauville Miami. February 16th, 1964

- She Loves You
- This Boy
- All My Loving

- I Saw Her Standing There
- From Me to You
- I Want to Hold Your Hand

☙❧

What Burt Reynolds Didn't Understand

One of the most questioned topics of President Carter's government was that of his relationship with Cuba in his attempt to bring both countries closer.

The White House issued a memorandum in April 1980, with the signature of President Jimmy Carter at the bottom, announcing that he would allow 3,500 Cuban refugees into the country. The Cuban government opened the Mariel port so that the exiles living in Florida could claim their families and friends. In the process, Castro took advantage of the opportunity and emptied the island's prisons, sending ships with a significant number of criminals and mentally ill. The final balance of refugees was 125,000. Twenty thousand people opted to live in Miami Beach and were joined by Haitians that took advantage of the open maritime borders. Life in Miami Beach changed overnight: It went from an 85,000-inhabitant city where less than 10% were Hispanic, to one whose Hispanic population rose to 23%. Street corners were filled with women selling their bodies and streets were filled with bullets and blood. Drugs sales were unleashed and reached the highest strata of society.

We met Ernest Stickley Jr. in *Swag*, a novel in which Elmore Leonard introduced him as an armed robber along with his partner Frank Ryan, a former car dealer. The duo will always be remembered for their peculiar way of stealing with a decalogue of rules created by themselves. The author didn't want to use the same character in his books, but Stickley Jr. was the exception: We saw him again in *Stick*, one of his first novels set in Miami after writing dozens in Detroit. This novel continues to find readers who place it among one of his most notable proposals. In *Stick*, Ernest Stickley Jr. is released after serving a seven-year sentence in Michigan and travels to Miami to meet Rainy, a Latin ex-convict and friend, to start a new life on the right track. But things get complicated in Miami when he finds out that Rainy, who gets killed in a shooting in the very first pages of the story, had businesses with some drug dealers.

Stickely gets involved with Miami's Anglo and Cuban mafia of the eighties, but not only marginally, as most of the works have portrayed. There are also mansions, tuxedo parties, convertibles, and even the deck of the Mutiny Hotel is mentioned more than once.

Two years after the book release came the movie. Directed by Burt Reynolds, who also played the role of Ernest Stickley Jr., it featured other starring roles played by Candice Bergen, George Segal and Charles Durning. Besides some interesting shots of the city – they filmed it from end to end: Everglades, Coconut Grove, Key Biscayne – *Stick* went from being a hard pulp novel with lots of action, that reflects the vice of Miami during the 80's to a movie with a glimpse of comedy. Limited to a sort of parade of implausible and grotesque characters and ridiculed by its costumes, it is very hard to follow during the two hours it lasts. Burt Reynolds failed to capture the meaning of the novel. Its characters are also grotesque, but they are never ridiculous. Quite the opposite. They are anti-heroes, created with great precision so that they can move comfortably in their sordid atmospheres. The movie does not recreate the context of the Cuban-American Mafia of that era, something that Leonard accomplishes very well.

It could be that Burt Reynolds didn't study Elmore Leonard´s work enough to understand his narrative universe. We are not certain about that, but the truth is that the film was classified by film critics as a total missense, and the narrator himself wrote these lines to Reynolds:

"When I'm writing I see real people and hear real people talking. But when I view the picture I see too often actors acting, actors hitting the wrong word, mugging, overstating or elaborating on a punchline, ad-libbing clichés, setting a record for the frequent use of "asshole." I hear what seem to me too many beats between exchanges, pauses for reactions, smiles for the benefit of the audience—like saying, "get it?"—or sneers or wide-eyed looks that I don't see in real life."

ဢ

Soundtrack

Many English and Spanish music bands have written songs about Miami. Among them: U2, Los Fabulosos Cadillacs, Will Smith, Counting Crows, John Mellencamp, Andrés Calamaro and Billy Joel. Loved and hated, The Magic City is not only a tourist attraction. It also attracts artists of all generations and genres.

The *Miami Vice* show's budget for music was ten thousand dollars. Yerkovich and Mann not only wanted to listen to unknown singer's covers and albums. They paid rights to the most important musical figures of the moment such as the Rolling Stones, Tina Turner, Phil Collins and Peter Gabriel in addition to having their own soundtrack. U2 joined the list of artists and one could see Crockett and Tubbs walking through Downtown or Miami Beach Marina or driving the black

143

convertible Ferrari through the MacArthur Causeway while "Pride (In the Name of Love)," "Wire," "Desire" and "Against Time" were playing in the background. But the connection between U2 and Miami didn't end there.

During that time, U2 was a renowned music band. One of the best. They left their imprint on the generation born during the 70s and later. By the eighties their albums: *Joshua Tree, War, Rattle and Hum* gave them worldwide recognition, and songs like "Where the Streets Have No Name," "Sunday Bloody Sunday" and "With or Without You" toured Europe, America and Asia as Billboard Top #1 songs. However, towards the nineties, the group sought to reinvent itself with a change of sound in their music and the look of its band members. The first songs of this new phase were *Zooropa* and *Achtung Baby*. That search brought them to Miami, to South Beach Studios, to record the most radical proposal of their career: *Pop*, a 12-song album with electronic, techno and rock rhythms. Pop was launched in 1997 and the result was not the best. It found many detractors and even the band was disappointed in it. Bono made a statement arguing they hadn't devoted the necessary amount of time for management due to reasons that were out of their control.

At some point they discussed that *Pop* should be called Miami, but that was just the title of one of the songs. During their recordings it became usual to see the four young Irish at Lincoln Road and Collins cafes and restaurants. They also recorded the Miami video which is a sort of postcard with a view to the ocean, elderly hanging around, efficiencies' facades and flowered shirts, all painted in light blue and pastel pink tones. It captures the local decadent essence of South Beach, a visual delight that is easy to imagine today at any corner of Meridian, Lexington or Pennsylvania avenues. Bono's Castro-style military outfit deserves special mention, since it may be unpleasant to the Cuban community.

The Miami song had worse luck than the album itself: Rolling Stone magazine, one of the most important landmarks in the musical context, described it as the worst song in the history of U2. Something similar happened at the local level: the Miami New Times and other media catalogued it as one of the five worst songs dedicated to the city of Miami. *"Often considered the worst U2 song ever written, it's hard to disagree. I give them points though for a good portrayal of South Beach circa mid-'90s. The song is as vapid and void of emotion yet oddly cool and glamorous like the South Beach we used to know and love. Also, seeing how this is a better portrayal of South Beach, the song should have been titled South Beach or at the very least Miami Beach. Because an accurate portrayal of Miami proper mid-'90s is urban wasteland filled with crackwhores and the homeless*

-- I guess that's still kind of true today." José, D. Durán.
Published in the *Miami New Times*, July 28, 2008.

Miami – U2, Pop.

Weather 'round here choppin' and changin'
Surgery in the air
Print shirts and southern accents
Cigars and big hair
We got the wheels and petrol is cheap
Only went there for a week
Got the sun got the sand
Got the batteries in the handy cam
Her eyes all swimming pool blue
Dumb bells on a diving board
Baby's always attracted to the things she's afraid of
Big girl with the sweet tooth
Watches the skinny girl in the photo shoot
Freshmen squeaky clean
She tastes of chlorine
My mammy
Love the movies, babe
Love to walk those movie sets
Get to shoot someone in the foot
Get to smoke some cigarettes
No big deal we know the score
Just back from the video store
Got the car and the car chase

What's he got inside the case
I want a close up of that face
Here comes the car chase
I bought two new suits
Miami
Pink and blue
Miami
I took a picture of you
My mammy
Getting hot in a photo booth
Miami
I said you looked like a madonna
You said maybe
Said I want to have your baby
Baby
Baby
We could make something beautiful
Something that wouldn't be a problem
We could make something beautiful
Something that wouldn't be a problem
At least not in Miami
You know, some places are like your auntie
But there's no place like
Miami
Miami
My mammy
Miami
Miami

About the Great Novel

*The debate on "Miami's great novel "in the Anglo
publishing sector is very divided. Russell Banks'
Continental Drift is considered one of the best candidates.*

One of the most prolific and prominent authors
of the American publishing sector is Russell Banks
(Massachusetts, 1940). Its trajectory —more than
twenty titles, including novels, stories, poems and
essays— has earned him the prestigious Dos Passos
Prize as well as numerous recognitions and some
screen adaptations.

Banks has two great, very complex and very
powerful books set in Miami: *Lost Memory of Skin*
(2011), which narrates The Kid's story, a sexual
predator in his early twenties who lives under a

bridge with others charged with the same offense, and *Continental Drift* (1985), which recounts two independent stories starring Bob DuBois and Vanise Dorsinville, on their journey to Miami — DuBois from within the country and Dorsinville from Haiti — each in search of a better life.

It is very likely that *Continental Drift* (Pulitzer finalist in 1999) is the most vast and ambitious novel written so far in terms of Miami literature. It introduces the reader to two immigrants who see Miami as the promised land; a recurring cliché today, but at that time it was new. But, like any great work, *Continental Drift* allows several readings: one is about the cultural clash between Anglo and Afro-Americans, another one is the human smuggling from Haiti and another one is about identity crisis.

DuBois emigrates from New England to an unexpected Miami in which he loses himself and his life compass. He declines and belittles himself. All this set in the 1980s, when Miami was a universe with abundant drugs, dirty businesses and violence.

Despite being published almost thirty years ago, *Continental Drift* represents Miami in full force: The issues addressed still appear on the ten o'clock TV headlines or on the front page of the newspapers.

Russell Banks, who lives six months in New York and the other six in Miami, was undoubtedly enmeshed by the charms and disenchantments of this city in order to recreate its fictions. His work reveals a narrator who knows the streets firsthand; he has inhaled them, he has felt them, and he is clear about the chaotic and interesting ethnic and cultural mosaic that is Miami. He is not like other authors from other cities or states who writes about the local context "without walking out of the airport."

It would be logical that novels like *Lost Memory of Skin* and *Continental Drift*, which represent the reality of a more Hispanic city, were textbooks for every Hispanic reader in Miami, but Russell Banks is not widely read in Spanish: Anagrama publishing company barely translated two or three of his books several years ago, which unfortunately are no longer found at the bookstores.

Continental Drift shouldn't only be appreciated and valued by American readers: for Hispanics, it should also be "Miami's great novel."

MEMORY
of SKIN

for Pedro Medina,
neighbor and
fellow-writer,
with best wishes,

[signature]

11/7/12

An Afternoon With Russell Banks
at the Panther Coffee
in South Beach

Talks with Mr. Banks, as I usually refer to him,
are always enriching.

Continental Drift is Miami's great novel. It was published
in 1985 and, until today, it represents the city just as it is.
Did you set out to describe the city in that book?

No. My inspiration came from a photo I saw in the
New York Times from some Haitians who had tried
to reach Miami illegally and lost their lives at sea.
That was during the spring of 1982. My idea was
to write a novel about immigration from within and
from outside the country.

And how did you come up with the idea of Bob DuBois, the other character who emigrated from New England to Miami?

At that time many people from other States immigrated to Florida. Bob DuBois is a typical hard-working, middle-class American from the middle states who must support his family with his salary. My family was like that, my father.

What was the hardest part to develop in Continental Drift?

The balance between the two stories. They're totally independent. While both are about immigration, they are completely different. I was afraid that one of them would prevail over the other one, so I had to find a balance. That was very difficult.

Did you do extensive research about Haitian culture to write Continental Drift?

I had read and investigated a lot about Haiti and its culture but not to write Continental Drift. I did it when I lived in Jamaica a few years, because I was interested in the topic.

In your books (Continental Drift and Lost Memory of Skin) you seem to have a lot of knowledge about the city.

How do you see Miami? What do you think of it?

I know the city very well, I love this city. I plan to die here. I came to Miami for the first time in 1959, then I came back in 1961 and I started living half time in New York and half time in Miami. I think Miami is the most American city there is right now. It's a land of immigrants and this is a country of immigrants. We should not forget that.

Although Continental Drift was not written with the purpose of describing the city of Miami, Miami is the novel's great character. What do you think about that?

I don't doubt that. Both *Continental Drift* and *Lost Memory of Skin* are stories that can only happen in Miami. They wouldn't be credible in any other place in the world.

In his book "Miami, City of the Future," T. D. Allman says he read Continental Drift and he loved it, but he didn't like the ending because it wasn't a happy one, and in Miami all endings are happy. What do you think about that?

All those who immigrate to Miami are looking for a happy ending, but very few have one — almost no one. In fact, life itself does not have a happy ending.

Miami is a tough, hard city. It has a happy ending for those who come to visit for a few days, because they go back to their home.

Miami in the 1980s, did you experience it closely? What can you tell us about it?

It was a very violent, dangerous city with a lot of dirty money. But above all, in those years I realized that the city was going to change, that the Anglo were going to lose power and the Latin American would gain it, because they were seizing Miami. And that is exactly what has happened. Now the Latinos are majority and, unlike California´s immigrants who occupy the lowest strata of society, Latin Americans here have power, money, they are involved in politics, they are entrepreneurs, they own banks.

It's impossible to talk about the nineteen eighties without mentioning the Miami Vice show. Were you interested in watching it?

Of course, I did. I loved it. I wrote the stories for some episodes. It was very important because it defined the city´s style. Miami was not like it was portrayed in the show, but it became so thanks to it.

The Dark Side of the Moonlight

The City of Miami was founded in 1896 and there is little information about its African-American culture to this day. However, these settlers have been one of the communities with greater presence. Creole is one of our main languages.

On February 26th, 2017, the *89Th edition of The Academy Awards* granted *Moonlight* with an Oscar for best film. Directed by Barry Jenkins and filmed in the Liberty City neighborhood of Miami, with a budget of just four million dollars, *Moonlight* tells the story of a character who, as a child, faces a sexual identity crisis in a quite hostile African American ghetto. Criticism has favored the film. It highlights, among its successes, that the cast is entirely African American and that exhibits a little-known face of Miami.

The first African-Americans who arrived in South Florida settled in Biscayne Bay and Coconut Grove. They emigrated from the Bahamas, fleeing poverty, to these prosperous farmlands. When Miami was founded as a city, more than 40% of its population came from the island and, despite its majority, the differences were soon very visible: African-Americans settled in colored Town — now known as Overtown — an area that created an imaginary frontier that was better not to cross. Hardieville, the first Red Light District of Miami, which was a cradle for gambling and prostitution, soon emerged there. In addition, black people were not allowed to do any work that the Anglos could do. The police force, with only white officers, had authorization to shoot any African-American who resisted arrest, and children did not have access to high school until 1926, since they were considered inferior beings. These differences were restrained until the Sixties, when the African-American community rioted the streets, creating the so-called *Miami riots*. They had more than twelve of those brawls, one of which, The McDuffie Case, left an indelible mark.

One of the darkest nights in Miami happened on the 17th of December 1979, as a prelude to the 1980′s riot. Arthur McDuffie, a 33-year-old black man, was driving a Kawasaki when an officer ordered him to stop, but he didn't. It is unknown why he did not comply with the officer's order and instead, tried to escape. A few minutes later he was arrested and beaten by over half a dozen policemen until his body was lying on the pavement, unconscious, convulsing and shedding blood through his scalp, nose, and cheekbones. Blood that drew chocolate colored stains on the asphalt. He died a few days later at Jackson Memorial Hospital.

The causes for the arrest and beating were never clarified, and the policemen involved were suspended and sued. At the hearing, which took place on May 17th, 1980, the prosecutor acquitted them, and a black mob soon went out into the streets of Liberty City to claim justice. Protests lasted 3 days and left 417 victims among the dead and wounded — mostly white. The riots wrecked homes, cars and shops, and closed schools.

Liberty City is still the most representative African-American neighborhood in Miami, followed by Opa Locka and a Coconut Grove area. The African-American community accounts for 20% of Miami's population, distributed between immigrants from Haiti, Jamaica and the Bahamas, the latter with predominance in terms of culture and religion. One of the community's most valuable legacies is the Charlotte Jane Memorial Park Cemetery, formerly called Coconut Grove Bahamian Park, where, as an urban legend tells, Michael Jackson recorded *Thriller*.

The Bee Gees American Dream

When everything seemed to indicate that the Bee Gees were going to say good bye the stage a last card came into play: Miami Beach.

On March 4, 2007, a ceremony was held in a small park in Miami Beach, on Purdy Avenue, overlooking the Venetian Causeway and the open sea of Biscayne Bay. Until then the park was named Island View Park, but since that day it would change to Maurice Gibb Memorial Park. Three years earlier, Maurice did not survive an intestinal obstruction surgery he went through at the Mount Sinai Hospital.

The Gibb brothers sealed a pact at a very young age. They swore they would become one of the greatest music bands in the world. Born in the United Kingdom, they emigrated to Australia when Barry, the eldest, was thirteen years old, and the twins Maurice and Robin were eight. Soon they began their musical adventures in school and with friends, then on stage and television. The album *The Bee Gees Sing and Play 14 Barry Gibb Songs* was released in 1965. Although it followed a stage of glory, Australia was not Europe or the United States. The roof was low and they had already reached it.

The Bee Gees returned to England in the late sixties. Robert Stigwood, Brian Epstein´s partner (who was the Beatles manager) was waiting for them with many expectations and a contract that only required their signatures.

In the beginning, the public was not indifferent, but they did not get to position themselves according to what was expected. The audience even threw eggs at the stage in one of their concerts. At that time the United Kingdom belonged to the Beatles, and if the Bee Gees wanted to emerge, they had to focus more on that style, both in music and lyrics, and steer away from their love songs. The group entertained the idea of separating, among many other ideas, but their friend Eric Clapton suggested they try their luck in America, in Miami. Clapton had confined himself to Miami Beach to recover from his heroin addiction, in a house on 461 Ocean Boulevard, near the Criteria Studios where he recorded Layla and prepared his next album, which had as title the address of the house and it's photo on the cover.

The Gibbs landed in Miami Beach to spend some time at 461 Ocean Boulevard. They also wanted to find a new style guided by producer Arif Mardin and Criteria Studios, which was a small mecca for musicians. Bob Dylan, the Eagles, Bob Marley, Fleetwod Mac, and James Brown had recorded for Atlantic Records there. The first single from the Bee Gees in Miami, *Jive Talkin*, was born in the SUV that took them through Biscayne, from Ocean Boulevard to Criteria, and showcased their new style, one with more rock rhythms which earned them Billboard's first place. The release of the album *Main Course*, with the themes "Winds of Change", "Fanny" and "Nights on Broadway" confirmed the quality of their new sound and established the change they sought. Then came the *Saturday Night Fever* soundtrack and their recognition as the greatest disco band in history.

In addition to *Main Course*, the Bee Gees recorded *E.S.P.* and *Spirits Having Flown* at

Criteria, which was, for most critics, the best of their work, with songs like "Tragedy" and "Too Much Heaven". The album took them to the Top #1 not only in the United States but also in England. By the late 70s and early 80s, the Gibbs family had already settled in Miami Beach, and in some interviews, when questioned why they had set up residence in this city, the answer was that they had fallen in love with Miami and its climate from day one

Tourists, Settlers and Adventurers in Latin America's Last Frontier

One of the few non-fiction books that have portrayed Miami in Spanish language is Miami. Turistas, colonos y aventureros en la última frontera de América, written by Argentinian journalist Hernán Iglesias Illa. A book that was ahead of its time but not published at the right time, and therefore went unnoticed. Even now, it's out of print.

Argentine journalist Hernán Iglesias Illa traveled to Miami for the first time in December 2003. For him — as for almost every intellectual and bohemian — culturally, the city represented the banal and the sordid paradigm, or as he mentions: "Miami was a black hole that swallowed humans calmly and joylessly, melting them in a bland and dull mash of hotels and shopping centers."

Iglesias did not arrive in Miami by his own volition. The telecommunications company he worked for sent him to a mobile phone congress. The first night of his trip he went to the bar at the Delano Hotel in South Beach and "he would never forget the drama, play and elegant imprint of that night." Little by little, he unveiled a city that had nothing to do with the Miami he had imagined— which is, surely, the same image of those who have never lived here. One afternoon, looking at the Art Deco houses on the Miami Beach streets, he thought that he could confine himself to writing the novel he had in mind in any of them.

That's where Iglesia´s relationship with Miami started. The city enticed a particular interest in him. He came back to the city half a dozen times and wrote the book *Miami. Turistas, colonos y aventureros en la última frontera de América Latina* as a result.

With optimal accuracy, the author works with essays, chronicles and the travel stories along the two hundred and twenty-three pages, giving the reader an x-ray vision of the city. Very well documented, it goes back to the origins of Miami to later penetrate through interviews and testimonies into what the city is today: a Latin American mosaic that has managed to impose itself on the Cuban exile.

With these variables, the author weaves what many of the inhabitants of Miami find in it: More than a city, a multifaceted phenomenon with an artificial paradise background.

In the book we discover a city that is tired of being known for its malls, beaches and bikinis. A city that encloses a cultural diversity as rich as any of the large metropolis like New York, London or Madrid, and where it is difficult to picture yourself in the long term, but not to seek immediate refuge. Above all, a city that, behind the Brickell and Biscayne buildings postcard, houses a huge population that is taking a risk at a new life opportunity.

Miami. Turistas, colonos y aventureros en la última frontera de América Latina should be a rigorous reading for all Miami inhabitants, the sort of reading we do with a notebook by our side. Besides bringing a little bit of the personal life of each of us who live here to its pages, it is an excellent source of information on history, social and cultural referents. If we could add something else it would be, perhaps, one or two "town's people testimonies" for the majority of those presented — though not all — are Jet Set, finance, politics and business icons. Even though, Hernán Iglesias has done a formidable job and has been able to capture those questions, frustrations and emotions that we, as "adventurers and settlers" carry as part of our baggage.

With Patricia Engel

New times in Miami expand the immigrant collage and literary voices emerge, refreshing the panorama and moving away from the noir genre.

···

Vida is a collection of short stories by Patricia Engel, a young American writer, daughter of Colombian immigrants and based in Miami. Engel is one of the most recognized *Latino* writers of the American publisher's circle and is also the author of *Veins of The Ocean* and *It's Not Love, It's Just Paris*. *Vida* is a handful of fairly uniform stories that develops between New Jersey, New York, Miami and Colombia. Its common denominator is the view of a central female character who lives among the contrast of cultures of who was born here, but whose roots are Latin American; one who invites you to a *pan de bono* while saying enjoy.

Because of the ease and fluency with which the stories are presented, it would seem that we are reading a light text, but that is not the case: we rather find ourselves in front of very accomplished stories. Engel has managed to reach the right balance between misery, irony and unease, to present conflicts such as the Anglo bias toward Latins, prostitution, illegality and drugs. Issues that, for those of us who walked Washington and Collins Avenue red sidewalks along with Engel and her characters, turns out to be our daily bread.

Engel's commitment to narrating these urban dramas — or maybe suburban dramas — has been quite risky, because the reality in which her fictitious universe feeds is so bewildering and unlikely that, if it´s not written properly, you run the risk of creating stories from clichés or absurdities, with characters that can escape the plausible. There is a long line of characters that parade through the pages of *Vida*: Argentines who sleep in the same room with eighteen roommates, Hungarians that supervise brothels, Peruvian-Japanese domestic helper girls, guitar teachers who, years ago, may have played with Mick Jagger — or someone just as famous as him — in addition to "Shula's," "Lucho," and "Maliks," who God only knows where they were born, but surely come from a different place in the world.

"Elsa is Ukrainian, a magnet for Russian guys, and within seconds she was showing off her Moscow slang to some guy named Vlad, who was handling flyers for the full Moon Party. Vlad pulled up a chair and then his friend showed up: A shirtless Argentinian — there are millions in South Beach.

Vida's stories moved me because they address everyday issues in the Latin underworld of the United States. Most of them are set in Miami, South Beach. Few authors have written these types of stories in this scenario, although it is true that this type of work is increasing.

We asked Ms. Engel if Latin literature was at it's best moment.

"I hope this is not its best moment yet, because right now there are just a few Latin voices raising their heads among an immense population," Ms. Engel paused. "I'm sure that this new stage of literature written by Latinos in the United States is increasing in strength every day. You must give it time. I feel very optimistic and excited when I think about the future of Latino artists and the ones that will come with our next generation."

☙

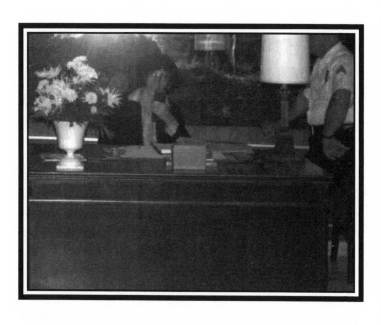

The Theft of the Century

The greatest jewel thief in the history of the United States was a surf champion who lived in Miami Beach.

Miami Beach quickly resurfaced from World War II and emerged as a waterfront metropolis. Winston Churchill spent a holiday there to brush off the aftermath of war. This renaissance gave way to the golden age of hotel industry and to a competition of luxury and glamour among the iconic Sans Souci, Fontainbleu and Eden Roc, easily won by the Fontainbleu.

Born from a whim of businessman Ben Novak in his desire to mint his own Modern French Provincial style — an adaptation of the French style for Miami Beach — the Fontainbleu is one of the

most mythical and legendary places of Miami. At the
time, it was the only hotel that had a nightly dress
code, ladies wore cocktail dresses and gentlemen a
suit and tie. It was Frank Sinatra's playground, where
he never paid even for a Coke, and his rooms were
privileged witnesses to the *affair* between John F.
Kennedy and Marilyn Monroe. But sometimes the
other side of opulence is crime, and the Fontainbleu
was constantly looted for jewelry and money, in spite
of the permanent security guards at its doors.

In 1955, Jack Roland Murphy arrived in Miami
Beach when he was 18, from the University of
Pittsburgh, Pennsylvania, tired of long winters and
snow, so different from the climate of his native
California. Murphy was tall, with a wide back and
well-defined angled factions. Besides being a refined
dandy, he was also a tennis and violin virtuoso and
a national surfing champion, trades of which he
taught classes, although his main job was at the
Poodle Room´s nightclub of the newly opened
Fontainbleu Hotel. This charming young man
gained popularity and affection under the nickname
of Murf the Surf. He soon noticed that the money
and jewels the guests kept in their rooms were a
small treasure that could finance his drinking nights
and women. We all know easy money never fills the
pocket, and the adventures of Murf soon went from

petty larceny to great embezzlement in the coastline mansions, in complicity with jewelry dealers. Murf, who spent hours at sea with his surfboard, knew the waters of Miami Beach. The holdups were made from his boat. He would drive the boat while his partners broke into the houses. He was even spotted at certain hotels in the Bahamas. However, the greatest robbery in history — as defined by justice —took place on October 29, 1964, at the American Museum of Natural History, New York, with Allan Kuhn, another Miami Beach playboy who was also a swimming instructor. Together they mocked security and alarms and stole JP Morgan´s jewelry collection, including the Blue Sapphire Star of India, the most valuable gemstone ever known. While the police had Murf under surveillance, at that time the hunt for criminals consisted of catching them red handed, and even though they failed to prove anything, a few days after the assault in New York the FBI broke into his house and found him and Kuhn with a couple of blondes and arrested them.

They were set free when they offered to return the jewels, cooperate with authorities and pay bail, but soon after they were arrested again. The sentence was only two years, and after being released Murf returned to Florida, an alcoholic who was addicted to marijuana. He murdered and mutilated a woman which earned him a life sentence, but luck was not elusive : He was saved from being executed in the electric chair and in 1986 he was granted freedom for good conduct.

While Murf was in prison, the film *Leave a Little Steal a Lot, The True Story of Murf the Surf* was released, set in the Splendorous Miami Beach of the sixties and their hotels, and visited by the Beatles and Muhammad Ali, whom he met personally. The film focuses on the Star of India theft, and according to Murf, it does not depict the truth.

Today, Murf dedicates his life to religion and visits prisons with his Bible guiding and converting convicts. He has promised to release information about his past for a documentary, but to date that has not happened

☙

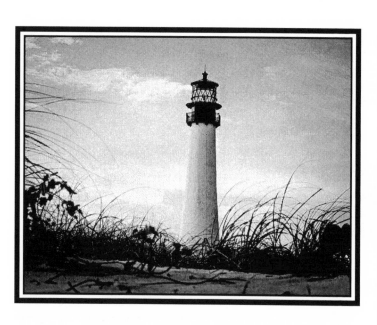

There Is A Light
That Never Goes Out

*The oldest structure in Miami Dade County is located
along Key Biscayne's oceanfront.*

It is known that the great discoveries of American lands
by the Spanish Crown are versions, accommodated for
textbooks, that little conform to reality. Florida is no
exception: it is known that Juan Ponce de León was not
the first to set foot in this territory, and there are those
who claim he never set foot in Saint Augustine. What
is clear is that Saint Augustine was the port of entry of
the first Portuguese sailors, long before Ponce de León
and the Spaniards. They were the ones who named it
Florida and later, under the promise of finding new
land, would travel by boat with hundreds of families to

settle down or explore southern horizons. Among those was a small island which Ponce de León called Santa Marta and later changed its name to Key Biscayne. That portion of land, more than four thousand years old, has witnessed how Florida has gone from English to Spanish hands and finally to Americans. As curious as it might appear, at the beginning it was not of great interest as a human settlement; however, its location made it a compulsory step for boats on route to Cuba or other islands of the Caribbean.

Florida became a part of the United States in 1821. Mary Ann Davis, a young, business-friendly woman, moved with her husband from Charleston, South Carolina, to Saint Augustine, where she bought the Key Biscayne acres under an incentive offer, at minimal cost. She made a proposal to the government to build a lighthouse to safeguard the navigation path which was getting increasingly dangerous due to piracy. There are many legendary Pirates on the east and west coasts of Florida. Such is the case of Spanish Juan Gaspar, in Tampa, whose legacy is the Gasparilla festival that takes place every year in January. The distinguished Sir Francis Drake, who docked on the shores of Key Biscayne at the service of the English kings, and Black Caesar, also in Biscayne Bay, a descendant of Africans feared for his courage and stature.

The project to build the *Cape Florida Lighthouse* easily got approval from Washington. It was lit December 13, 1825 and remained lit until 1835, when a hurricane caused severe floods that damaged its structure, which fortunately was quickly repaired. The government's interest in the *Cape Florida Lighthouse* went beyond providing security for the navigators. The *Lighthouse* was essential to attract villagers to the area, and thus take another step in the displacement of native Indians, Seminoles, with whom they were at war to strip them of their territory. They had almost managed to minimize the Seminoles to some specific points like the Everglades. The Seminole Wars have been one of the most costly and bloody battles the United States waged internally. It started in Pensacola, but it spread throughout the state and lasted more than forty years. Among noted episodes, in addition to the decapitation of one of its leaders, the Osceola Chief, we have the attack on the *Cape Florida Lighthouse* on July 23rd, 1836, which went on through the whole night and claimed the life of one of the guards. It also caused major damage which forced its closure, suspending operations for an indefinite time and shielding the perimeter with military bases – Fort Dallas, perhaps the best known.

For eleven long years the *Cape Florida Lighthouse* remained unlit until the renovation work began. Then it lit up the road intermittently until 1996, when it finally turned off its light.

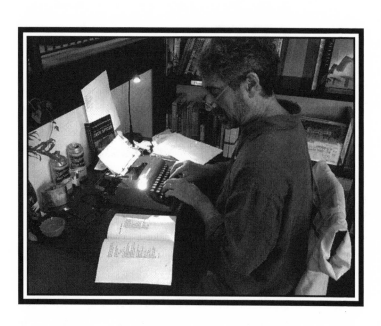

Our Quixote

The mastermind of one of the most important independent bookstores in the United States and the country's largest Book Fair is a Miami born who left law school and followed his dream of selling books.

The National Book Foundation Award Ceremony was held at the Cipriani restaurant in New York on November 16th, 2011. It was a tuxedo and long tablecloth dinner where Mitchell Kaplan was awarded the highest accolade for his work in support of the United States literature: *Outstanding Service to the American Literary Community*. In the acceptance speech, Kaplan, very elegant but still bearing his somewhat scruffy look: disheveled and unshaven, made an emotional recount of his life since he decided to undertake the adventure of selling books more than thirty-five years ago. He also thanked his family, present at the event, and the Books & Books team.

The biggest problem that Miami faced in 1982 was eradicating violence and cocaine consumption and sales. This had overtaken Miami. The city was also in transition in which the Anglo population was leaving the city giving way to an increasingly growing Latin American community. The Mariel exodus was barely over and that made things even more difficult. Also, in 1982, a 25-year-old boy who had faced a vocational crisis decided to take control of his life looking into different venues; he left law school in Washington and returned to Miami, his hometown, with a unique and firm purpose: selling books. That was the beginning of Mitchell Kaplan´s journey with Books & Books, one of the most important independent bookstores in the country and the most important one in Miami. Not only for its wide range in Spanish and English books, but because it is one of the most important incentives in cultural activity and management. This has led to a strong community of readers, publishers and authors in both languages. His first shop, where Joan Didion took refuge when writing her book *Miami*, was in Coral Gables, on Aragon Avenue, almost in front of the actual one. A small area with wooden shelves arranged from floor to the ceiling, with the same charm that characterizes Books & Books until today. Back then, Kaplan alternated between being a bookseller and a high school English teacher, but he didn't have to do it for long: In that old Miami it was easier to meet certain economic goals.

Kaplan's vision of Miami – this has been mentioned on other occasions – was not so alien to the one of those who felt that this city needed to be vindicated, although his battle was different: He waged it from culture, from literature, from the books.

A year after he opened Books & Books he created the Coral Gables literary and writer festival. But Mitchell Kaplan was not the only one who saw potential in Miami or wanted to revendicate it. Dr. Eduardo Padrón, at that time Miami Dade College's Wolfson campus Director (actually he is the President of Miami Dade College), wanted to organize a literary festival at the College and asked Kaplan to join forces and talent. The first edition of the Miami Book Fair was held in 1984 under the name Books by the Bay. It lasted two days and summoned more than seventy writers and twenty-five thousand people. Over time, it has managed to consolidate as the largest and most important book fair in the country. With a budget of more than one and a half million dollars, the most prominent exponents of English and Spanish literature have participated in it, reuniting more than six hundred writers in its latest edition of 2018.

A lot of water has gone under the bridge since Kaplan started his journey. Now it is a local, national and international reference, showing up in the directories of the most relevant cultural entities. Its prizes and recognitions are countless. It is common to find him in the acknowledgements section of English language books written by Miami authors, and yet, just as in the beginning, he sits at the Books & Books Cafe with his cup of coffee or a glass of water and disheveled hair.

❧

Woodstock in Front of the Sea

*The idea of the greatest music festival of all times in the
United States was conceived in Miami.*

On the afternoon of May 18th, 1968, Mothers of
Invention, Frank Zappa's band, closed their repertoire
at the Gulfstream Race Track of Hallandale Beach
to twenty-five thousand people. Many of them,
students from different states who shared joints over
the blankets spread over the grass. The best would
come afterwards: Jimi Hendrix, wearing a tight white
shirt and red trousers, slid down from a helicopter
with his band, and landed on the stage.

Although in 1960s Miami was a budding, far-
right and conservative city, it was not indifferent to
the counter-cultural movement that had so much

strength in San Francisco and New York. Back then Coconut Grove was an artist's village and young boys with long hair, wispy beards and flared trousers that listened to folk music and peacefully protested in favor of human rights and against the Vietnam war. Among them was Michael Lang, a New York music lover who locked himself in his room to smoke marijuana since he was 14 while listening to John Coltrane or Celia Cruz. At sixteen he tried unmatched sensory trips with LSD. That same summer, an older African American woman who wore high heels and elegant evening dresses, introduced him to a world that would end up changing his life: The Bohemian and counter-culture of the Village. When he finished high school, he moved to the Village, where he surrounded himself with artists, creators and musicians. He attended New York University (NYU), although he never hung the diploma on his wall. Before graduating he dropped out of school, sold what he had and left with his girlfriend on a road-Trip to Miami, to Coconut Grove, the neighborhood he knew that caught his attention. Lang's plan was to open a Smoke-shop and, although the first attempt in South Miami failed because the police intervened right at the inauguration and closed it for not having a license, the second try in Coconut Grove was different.

Lang's new store was named The Head Shop South. Walls lined with Dylan, Allen Ginsberg, Lenny Bruce posters and The Beatles, Rolling Stones and The Byrds playing loud on the speakers. The back room operated as the underground newspaper *The Libertarian Watchdog* and became a party time spot to smoke marijuana and LSD trips. Seizing the moment, Lang began organizing concerts in venues such as the Coconut Grove Dinner Key Auditorium, where Jim Morrison was involved in a scandal already mentioned. These concerts consolidated him and his shop as one of the main references of the Counterculture in Miami. But his biggest, major project was brewing in his own kitchen, along with a group of friends and colleagues: the first music festival in Florida history. Little by little the project took shape and the Miami Pop Festival was created. Set at Gulfstream Race Track, it would last a weekend and the guest list included Miami bands and other great musicians like John Lee Hooker, Chuck Berry, Mothers of Invention, Blue Cheer, Crazy World of Arthur Brown and Jimi Hendrix, who was touring the country and playing his last concert there, thus the helicopter entrance.

The first day, Saturday, was a resounding success, 'It Was Magic,' said Lang. However, on Sunday, Miami's tropical climate with its rains and winds took over and the event was cancelled almost right after starting. The artists withdrew to their hotels and on the way back, while in his limo, Hendrix composed "Rainy Day, Dream Away."

Michael Lang incurred a large amount of debts to create the Miami Pop Festival, and the cancellation of the second date did not allow him to pay them back. He chose to file for bankruptcy, pack his things and return to New York, to Woodstock, a village surrounded by mountains that had become a small mecca for musicians and artists with the purpose of replicating their idea of Florida. And the following summer, he produced Woodstock –and the rest is history.

ॐ

City of All, City for All.

Around the year 2000, a new chapter in the history of Miami's Latin American community began to be written. The city grows and claims that the American dream has full validity.

The migratory waves of the late nineties, with a high prevalence of Venezuelans, Argentinian, Brazilians and Colombians, came to replicate the Middle- or upper-middle-class life model they left behind. The city has grown since then: downtown, with its imposing aquamarine glass towers, the artists quarter in Wynwood and the periphery with its uniform flan-colored Townhouses and double fall terracotta roofs.

Throughout history, Miami has demonstrated that it is not afraid of change and rather knows how to adapt to it. Now we can talk about a large sociocultural change that has a clear manifestation in the art and culture produced and consumed in the city, like the musicians who never thought — nor did we —would be able to play guitar for the Miami audience.

In 2011, four singer-songwriters played for the first time in Miami: Manu Chao, Pablo Milanés, Andrés Calamaro and Joaquín Sabina. Pablo Milanés visit transcended the artistic level and created controversy among the Cuban exile, which opposed it radically. But this city is suitable to all and, like it or not, Milanese's Trova is listened to and admired in a massive way in Latin America. Therefore, it was not a surprise to see thousands of teary fans at the American Airlines Arena, especially when he played Éxodo, dedicated to the Cubans that, for different reasons, have abandoned the island.

Art is not imperialist or communist, neither does it understand about nationalities. Art is art and, and although it sounds like a cliché, that was more or less Sabina's message, who also caused some controversy when he played at the American Airlines Arena and excused himself for not visiting us during almost 30 years. However, at a press conference he argued that people did not want him here and therefore they did not invite him, and exactly the same happened to his friend and brother Pablo Milanés.

Calamaro had already been seen in Miami, in ocean front hotels or with shopping bags strolling by Lincoln Road. He even wrote a chronicle years ago on his blog, where he compared Miami to a middle-class elephant graveyard. He recorded songs from his album *Honestidad brutal* here, and in an interview, he was disgusted because he couldn't smoke a joint, but he never offered a solo concert —yes, at another time with *Los Rodríguez*— his tour, Still Alive and Well, alluding to his recent fiftieth birthday, played in Las Vegas, New York, Chicago and Miami Beach´s Fillmore.

The sky at Bayfront Park in downtown Miami was clouded with marijuana smoke the night Manu Chao arrived with the Tour de la Ventura, a sold out show that promised a lot but accomplished little. His appearance on the stage was very conservative, which wasn't that bad at the start, but the mood did not change, and the audience experienced a distant and alienated artist through the whole concert. Manu Chao probably got on the stage with the "Miami cliché" in his head. The one that places it as a frivolous and shallow city, and he didn't consider that he would be standing before a huge group of seasoned "expatriates" that would have enjoyed a little more of a ghetto Manu, true to his style: "Ya llegó, ya llegó lo peor de la rumba. Ya llegó, ya llegó, el Manu Chao."

porno.com

*Mark Zuckerberg, Daniel Ek, Chad Hurley, Steve Chen and
Jawed Karim, creators of Facebook, Spotify and YouTube,
are considered contemporary geniuses. Their contributions
changed the world and the industry. Kristopher Hinson's
name should also be added to that list; from the streets of
Miami Beach, he reinvented one of the most consumed
elements in current popular culture: Pornography.*

———————

At the age of twenty, Verónica Rodríguez worked
behind a McDonald's counter and lived in a garage.
Her skin had a cinnamon tone, her proportions
were delicate, and her features and smile made her
look younger. She had immigrated from Venezuela
not too long ago with her mother and, as it usually
happens during the adaptation process, money was
short way before the end of the month. But her life

experienced a radical change when a client offered her to participate in a porn video. It was a secondary role for a web portal. It was not bad, even more so considering that it was Bang Bros, the industry's best. Then there would be major roles in that and many other of the most important websites. In her first year, Verónica earned nearly one hundred thousand dollars. She closed her fourth year with more than four hundred thousand.

The internet arrived at the end of the nineties and the beginning of this new century, and with it the Dot-com business fever that created web companies with no moderation. Most of them disappeared sooner than later or went broke. By 2002 the virtual stage was better established, and although we didn't have a computer in every room, internet became a family member. That's when Kristopher Hinson and Penn Davis, University of Florida students, moved to Miami. They set up a tinted glass van with a camera and began recruiting young couples to have sex in exchange for a few dollars and then they uploaded the videos to the net, at the Bang Bus domain.

Until that time, the epicenter of the pornographic industry was concentrated in the West Coast, between California and Nevada. It was an inaccessible world of lush blondes, exclusive studios and high production costs marketed through DVDS. Hinson, the project's mastermind, had the premise that people could run out of work, be homeless, go days without eating, get expelled from school, but could not stop masturbating. The Bang Bus approach bearded the amateur porn tag and was the absolute opposite to the Californian model: low budget, homemade performers that ranged from McDonalds' Latin cashiers to college students. However, the sex van had to drive through Brickell, Ocean Drive and Washington Avenue to enhance the contrast of its decadence against Miami's glamour. The Bang Bus views and subscriptions grew exponentially from the start — some videos generated earnings of up to fifty thousand dollars a month. Today it has thirty-six sister pages operating under the Bang Bros umbrella, with participating stars like Ron Jeremy, Kendra Lust and Sandra Romain. Besides, it is still a beginner's showcase, like Verónica Rodríguez was back in the day. Now she is considered a porn star and has over two hundred scenes on multiple platforms.

While Bang Bus is still one of the leaders and its website is valued at over sixty-six million dollars, nowadays it's just one more option within an infinite offer — today, anyone with a camera shoots adult content in their room.

Nearly 30% of U.S. pornography is produced in Florida —The West Coast ceased to be the Mecca and now it's Miami, and lush blondes look for opportunities in Miami Beach — and massively consumed online through paid memberships, webcams, social networks or trailers played in WhatsApp and unloaded while waiting for the traffic light to change.

જી

David & Goliath

Can David Beckham and his soccerl team give Miami the recognition the city was looking years ago in Major League Soccer (MLS)?

In December 1993, the draw for the US World Cup teams was held in Las Vegas, Nevada. It was a long distance to travel to host the most important game of soccer. The main obstacle was its minimal relationship with the sport. However, USA 94 was the world's most watched cup in history. It boasted a crowd of 3,568,567 and an average 68.6 spectators per game, followed by Germany in 2006 and Brazil in 2014. One of the commitments that the United States promised in order to be the host country was to create a greater and more competitive soccer league, so, on that same winter afternoon in Las

Vegas, they announced the launch of Major League Soccer (MLS).

MLS started in 1996 with 10 teams. In 1998, two more were added. One of them was the Miami Fusion, a strategic bet to consolidate the project for the great Hispanic community of South Florida. The owner was investor Ken Horowitz. The team played at the Orange Bowl stadium at first, but then Joe Carollo, Miami´s mayor, retracted that offer. Horowitz's search for a new space brought him to Lockhart High School in Fort Lauderdale, where he faced several limitations. The main obstacle was seating capacity for only seven thousand people, which was expanded to house twenty thousand. Next was the problem of recruiting a big star that could attract fans. Horowitz hired Colombian star Carlos "El Pibe" Valderrama, who was playing for the Tampa Mutiny at that time. El Pibe, who wore his teams' uniform in USA 94 and whose name echoed among the bleachers, was presented as one of the best players in the world. The Fusion debut was not very good, nor was its general performance, so they closed ranks at 2001. Among the various reasons attributed to their failure were inadequate support from administration, hot, rainy and humid weather, the stadium not having the required capacity and no ticket stands. Ticket purchases were handled from a customized trailer.

In 2018, Miami is about to write a new soccer chapter thanks to David Beckham. After years of negotiation with the city and MLS, Beckham has managed to incorporate the "International Soccer Club of Miami" into the league for 2020. The stadium location, as with the Fusion, seems to be a problem. Several places want to host. During the nineties attempt with the MLS, the city was dominated by Latin Americans, a very different profile from the city today. The previous Miami inhabitants were immigrants from Cuba and Central America, countries that were foreign to soccer. Contemporary Miami is also the immigrant capital of America´s southern cone, whose inhabitants are all soccer fans. It´s a small Argentina, a small Brazil and a large Colombia. In contemporary Miami, the World Cup and the Copa América are games that must be seen from the very beginning, with the feverish exchange of "Panini album stamps" at Walgreens and gas stations, and the community wearing various team uniforms at once. The joy lasts from the opening ceremony up to the last game. Even Croatian audiences watched the Russian final. The Barça and Real Madrid are not foreign to these celebrations either, each time they play a classic, or one of them is playing the Champions final, the streets turn into a parade of blaugrana (blue and red) and meringue T-shirts. And meanwhile, the indoor soccer fields are proliferating in Doral, Brickell, Midtown and Kendall.

The bonds that the average immigrant almost never cuts with his country are food and soccer. Every Sunday they visit specific restaurants to order traditional meals, and no matter how many years ago they emigrated, they continue to be fans of Boca, River, Medellín National, Alianza Lima, Junior of Barranquilla and many more. If you still like other teams those probably are Barcelona and Madrid. What the Inter Miami will have at the beginning will be fans, not "hinchas", and the teams supports the demands of their "hinchadas", not the eventual Saturday night hinchas. Beckham has told the media that his team will offer the best, even Messi and Cristiano Ronaldo together. Hopefully it will do so, helping Miami regain soccer popularity. Of course, this is David Beckhams proposal. The public will have the last word.

☙

Books & Libro's

The Spanish literature written in Miami is claiming its place and leads the native production, the United States production, in our language. Writer and academic Naida Saavedra has coined the term #NewLatinoBoom and positions Miami as the leader of the new trend.

Since a few years ago there is a tacit commitment in Miami to vindicate Spanish literature: a sort of exalted response against those who see in Miami a bland and artificial city. Without noticing, this has created a small literary ecosystem that certainly tends to evolve. In Miami we have the largest Spanish-language book fair in the country. The same thing applies for bookstores, as is the case of Altamira, publishing companies, magazines, a literary and cultural agenda for all tastes, and authors with certain common codes are starting to surface.

Do we have literary works that we could catalog as from Miami? The writing by local authors has a particular record. It must be clear: none of the Miami writers left their country to come here and become a writer. Nevertheless, it's happening today with New York and other cities that offer creative writing in Spanish. Miami writers have fled from political, economic, or abusive government crises. For obvious reasons, during the early years in the city — five on average — their biggest concern was burying the past, getting their immigrant status, getting a job, cutting old ties and creating new ones. After solving that complex equation, they began to write with the idea of making a career in literature. And we must look closely at this literature, because it is a different proposal and, until now, it has been seldom exposed. They are literary works with common references in which Miami is forcefully present, denoting the author's urgency to describe a city that stands in contrasts to its sweet outline, describing it as marginal, violent and cosmopolitan. They have a language of their own that is neither Spanglish nor the Spaniard Spanish left behind by the author when he left his country years ago. It's a blend of Cuban, Colombian, Venezuelan, Argentinean, Peruvian and Mexican that absolutely breaks all schemes of academic acceptance but, in the context of Miami, is more plausible than any other. In literature, novelty contributes plenty, and we are witnessing something extremely innovative.

But we must remain objective: this is just beginning; the city's storytellers still have a lot to prove. Until now, the "Miami's great novel" title remains vacant. Perhaps, for now, if we had to talk about a novel in Spanish that represents or better defines the city, we should read *Nieve sobre Miami*, by Spaniard author Juan Carlos Castillón, although it is a work written from —and set in— a very premature Miami. Some argue that *Boarding Home*, by Guillermo Rosales, is Miami's great novel in Spanish, but although Rosales's book is brutal and powerful, it does not define the city and may well happen in any other geographic area.

Here's a brief list of books to keep in mind:

Spanish, fiction

Not necessarily all the books in this list have been of my liking—even their literary quality can be debated —but setting that aside, I think each one has something interesting to show or say about Miami. Each one describes its author's view of Miami. By the way, this list— like all lists — is arbitrary and limited to the knowledge of the author. Also, he acknowledges that, most surely, many other literary works been left out.

- *Nieve sobre Miami*, Juan Carlos Castillón (Spain).
- *El círculo del alacrán*, Luis Zalamea (Colombia).
- *Little Havana. Memorial Park*, Eduardo Leandro Campa (Cuba).
- *Viaje One Way*, anthology of stories edited by Hernán Vera Álvarez (Argentina) and Pedro Medina León (Perú).
- *Jáspora*, Carlos García Pandiello (Cuba-Venezuela).
- *Vida*, Patricia Engel (Colombia, recently translated to Spanish).
- *Volver a morir*, Rosana Ubanell (Spain).
- *El ocaso, Andrés* Hernández Alende (Cuba).
- *Miss Blues 104ºF*, Jaime Cabrera (Colombia).
- *La clarividente de la Calle Ocho*, Anjannete Delgado (Puerto Rico).

Spanish, non-fiction

- *Miami. Turistas, colonos y aventureros en la última frontera de América Latina*, Hernán Iglesias Illa (Argentina).
- *Miami [Un]plugged. Crónicas y ensayos personales de una #CiudadMultigutural*, anthology, edited by Hernán Vera Álvarez (Argentina) and Pedro Medina León (Perú).

- *Extremo Occidente*, Juan Carlos Castillón (Spain).

In addition, there are three essential non-fiction books in English that help you understand the city and should be compulsory reading: *Miami, City of the future*, T. D. Allman; *Black Miami in the Twentieth Century*, by Marvin Dunn; and *Going to Miami*, by David Rieff. The first one was entirely the culprit of my increasing interest in this, my new home.

❧

Afterword: or Requiem for Another Lost Country

This book, as with many other books, has no ending.

There was an attempt against Nicholas Maduro, the Venezuelan dictator, the week I was reviewing the final version of this manuscript. It was Saturday, August 4th, at a military parade and they used explosive drones. Among the multiple theories about the origin of the attack and its perpetrators, and even its veracity, because for many it was a hoax from the same regime, Peruvian journalist Jaime Bayly affirmed on his Late Night Show that he was aware of it beforehand. It was not a farce. He had met with one of the conspirators who gave details of what was in store for the dictatorship and its cupola. Bayly's show is a trench against the abusive regime of Miraflores, and although his position is controversial because outsiders believe his statements have made him look like an accomplice to the assassination, he has innumerable endorsers and supporters in South Florida.

Miami's different periods are easy to identify. Its history is brief. We have the foundational period, the Anglo, the 80's, the touristic, the mafia, the Cubans, the Latin Americans and, for some time now, the Venezuelans. I arrived in Miami in 2002, when Hugo Chávez was already in office. Back then, the ones behind the counters carrying trays full of dirty dishes were not Venezuelan. They were Argentineans, Peruvians, Colombians, Bolivians, and all those who comprised the "Latin American Miami." But now, besides being a majority in those jobs and driving nine out of ten Ubers, there are thousands who come to replicate the high or middle high class life model they left behind. That is why Miami is filled with entrepreneurs, investors, journalists, chefs, and artists scattered in the Doral – Doralzuela – and Weston – Westonzuela – both noble neighborhoods.

The Caracas satrapy has created a scattered puzzle between New York, Miami, Buenos Aires, Lima, Spain and Colombia. In Miami, however, it seems as if a previous episode is being rewritten. In his book *Flight 495*, Colombian journalist Gerardo Reyes defines Miami as a "Conspiracy City" for its barrack quality. Plans to overthrow the governments of Somoza, Castro, and Chávez have been plotted here. Cuba is in Miami´s DNA, so the plans of the CIA with Cuban exiles Ricardo Morales, Rafael Villaverde and Carlos Quezada, drug traffickers and leading gangsters in that no-man's land at the deck of the Mutiny Hotel, are subjects of entire chapters in our history books.

It is a reality that there are hundreds of immigrants from the land of Bolívar arriving in Miami on a daily basis with their arepas, cocosetes, panas, chamos, nostalgia, frustrations and affections, transforming it socially and culturally more than any other American community. Just as it is a reality that rebel groups are concentrated in Miami with the support of the intelligence service of this country, a public secret, plotting to overthrow Maduro. However, it is premature to talk about the Venezuelan Miami with specific details. We started talking about the Cuban Miami twenty or twenty-five years after the Cubans settled here. Surely, in a few years, we will have a new chapter on Miami´s road map: the Venezuelan chapter, with names and surnames that will be branded as heroes or terrorists according to the viewer. With dates, facts, traditional and emblematic restaurants, and hopefully, the triumph of the rebel and conspiring opposition.

This book, as with many other books, has no ending.

About The Cover

To be an artist, according to Claudio Roncoli, is to make the invisible visible and to be free and committed to his work but more importantly not to repeat itself. Perhaps that is why it is difficult to define and classify his work. We could find his murals in the streets of Wynwood or Brickell or see him at the Grammy awards ceremony raising the highest award for the cover of a music album he has designed. We can also see his work at an art gallery where his paintings are exhibited.

Claudio was born in Argentina and lives in Miami where he has his atelier. Although he spends time in New York, Latin America and Asia with his projects *Black Life*, *Empty Project* and *Life*. The bond between Claudio and music is close. We saw this between 2013 and 2014 in his work *Rock saved my life*, a sort of tribute to the bands and mythical musicians who inspired him. At the age of eight, his brother introduced to him his first vinyl album of Kiss. The cover shows the band members falling off a cliff.

Claudio is currently preparing the aesthetic and visual concept of a new album with four musician friends. Another of his interests is writing.

roncoliart.com

@claudioroncoli @claudioroncoli Claudio Roncoli

About the author

Pedro Medina León is an award winning author, speaker and editor. He is the author of the acclaimed novel Varsovia (Florida Book Award 2017), Mañana no te veré en Miami, Marginal and Tour: una vuelta por la cultura popular de Miami, and editor of the anthologies Viaje One Way and Miami (Un) Plugged. Medina León is a speaker member of the Florida Humanities Council for the 2018 –2019 program, and co-creator of the Escribe Aquí Festival, for the Betsy Hotel, which was awarded with a grant from the Knight Foundation and frequently gives talks around the country on writing, reading, and multiculturalism. In 2008 he created the cultural portal Suburbano Ediciones today suburbano.net is the leading Spanish-Language cultural network in the United States. He also is a contributing columnist for El Nuevo Herald and studied Literature at Florida International University.

Acknowledgements

To JJ. Colagrande, Gastón Virkel, Hernán Vera Álvarez and Diana Cornejo, for readings and comments. To Elizabeth, for the needed space. To Isabella, my direct contact with 305. To Gustavo Lombardo, for all his support.

Credits

Our Man in Miami
Puente Old Seven, by Cbdehart.
Creative Commons Attribution Share.

The Briefest Concert
Mugshot, Jim Morrison. Archives Dade County Public Safety
Department.

Al Capone was the first
Mugshot, Al Capone. Miami Police Department Archive.

Tropical Bagdad
City Hall, Opa Locka City, by Ebyabe.
Creative Commons Attribution Share.

A Big House in the Jungle
Panoramic view if Vizcaya, by Rob Pinion

The most glam murder
FBI most wanted ad. Public Domain.

Lon Life Scarface
Mural Design District de Miami. Picture by Redleaf.
Creative Commons Attribution Share

Woodstock in front of the sea
The Jimi Hendrix Experience. Creative Commons.

During War Times Miami is a Trench
Postcard. Public Domain.

Calle Ocho
Author's picture

Charming Man
Richard Dening y Patricia Crowley, characters de la serie Michael Shayne. Creative Commons Attribution Share

When the Snow Covered Us.
Ocean Drive. Creative Commons Attribution Share

The Literature District
George E. Merrick. Creative Commons Attribution Share.

The Dark Side of the Moonlight
Mural de Martin Luther King Jr, by Oscar Thomas, en el barrio de Liberty City. GNU Free Documentation License.

The G.O.A.T.
Muhammad Ali y Malcolm X, picture by EPHouston. Creative Commons Share Attribute.

La Folie
Authors Picture.

People of the future.
Authors Picture.

The Great Masacre
Creative Commons Share Attribute.

porno.com
Verónica Rodríguez. picture Michael Dorausch,
www. michaeldorausch.com

Patricia Engel
Picture by Elliot & Erick Jimenez.

Soundtrack
Picture by David Shankbone, under the License of Creative Commons Attribution Share.

Lyrics of Miami: *Universal Music Publishing Group. Written by Adam Clayton, Dave Evans, Larry Mullen and Paul Hewson.*

Additional Pictures and Images:
http://ar.fotolia.com

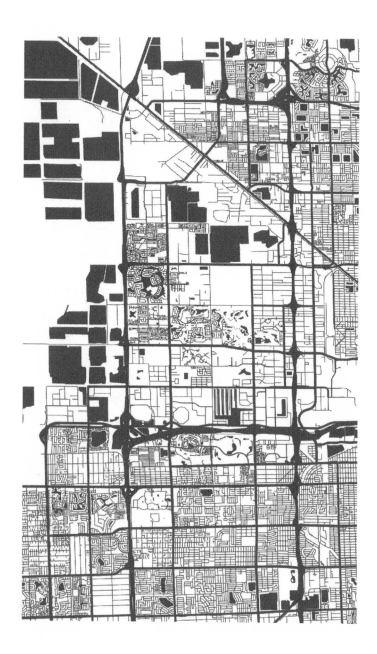

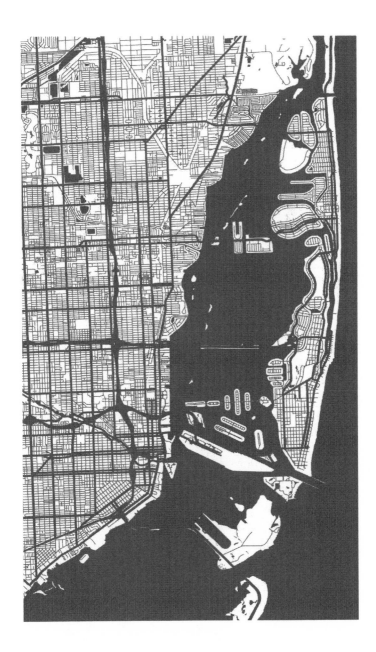